The Psychology of Personnel Selection

In many companies the procedures for selecting the right person for the job are little more than a lottery. Optimal personnel selection is concerned with accurately predicting employees' future behaviour in the job.

Drawing on recent scientific research, this book offers a 'framework for action' to assist selectors in this difficult task. Based on the principles of Total Quality Management, topics include identifying customer needs, establishing the necessary evaluative standards for all selection methods, optimizing the design and return on investment in selection procedures, setting decision-making standards, and outlining ideas for continuous improvements. Many selection methods are also described and discussed in relation to the evaluative standards.

The benefits to be gained from the framework reside in the systematic matching of people to jobs. The framework also provides a means with which to monitor and assess the efficacy of the overall selection procedure. This framework should enable the selection decision-makers to predict someone's future job performance with much greater accuracy. This, in turn, will help their company to survive, prosper and grow.

Dominic Cooper is Director of Applied Behavioural Sciences Ltd, Hull. **Ivan T. Robertson** is Professor of Occupational Psychology, and Head of Manchester School of Management, UMIST.

ESSENTIAL BUSINESS PSYCHOLOGY

Series editor: Clive Fletcher

This series interprets and examines people's work behaviour from the perspective of occupational psychology. Each title focuses on a central issue in management, emphasizing the role of the individual's workplace experience.

Other books in the series:

The Healthy Organization
Ethics and Diversity at Work
Sue Newell

Business Leadership
Viv Shackleton

Impression Management in Organizations
Paul Rosenfeld, Robert A. Giacalone and Catherine A. Riordan

The Psychology of Personnel Selection

A *Quality Approach*

Dominic Cooper and Ivan T. Robertson

London and New York

First published 1995
by Routledge
11 New Fetter Lane, London EC4P 4EE

Simultaneously published in the USA and Canada
by Routledge
29 West 35th Street, New York, NY 10001

Typeset in Times by Solidus (Bristol) Limited
Printed and bound in Great Britain by
Biddles Ltd, Guildford and King's Lynn

British Library Cataloguing in Publication Data
A catalogue record for this book is available from the British Library

Library of Congress Cataloguing in Publication Data
A catalogue record for this book has been requested

ISBN 0–415–13081–6 (hbk)
ISBN 0–415–10326–6 (pbk)

— *Contents*

—— *Figures*

—— *Tables*

Series editor's preface

The rapid, far-reaching, and continuing changes of recent years have brought about a situation where understanding the psychology of individuals and teams is of prime importance in work settings. Organizational structures have shifted radically to the point where individual managers and professionals have far greater autonomy, responsibility and accountability. Organizations seek to reduce central control and to 'empower' individual employees. Those employees combine in teams that are frequently cross-functional and project-based rather than hierarchical in their construction. The traditional notion of careers is changing; increasingly, the expectations is that an individual's career is less likely to be within a single organization, which has implications for how organizations will command loyalty and commitment in the future. The full impact of the information technology revolution is finally being felt, with all the consequences this has for the nature of work and the reactions of those doing it.

The capacity of people to cope with the scale and speed of these changes has become a major issue, and the literature on work stress bears testimony to this. The belief in the importance of individuals' cognitive abilities and personality make-up in determining what they achieve and how they can contribute to team work has been demonstrated in the explosive growth in organizations' use of psychometric tests and related procedures. Perhaps more than ever before analysing and understanding the experience of work from a psychological perspective it is necessary to achieve the twin goals of effective performance and quality of working life. Unfortunately, it is the latter of these that all too often seems to be overlooked in the concern to create competitive, performance-driven, or customer-focused cultures within companies.

It is no coincidence that the rise in the study of business ethics and increasing concern over issues of fairness paralleled many of the organizational changes of the 1980s and 1990s. Ultimately, an imbalance between the aims and needs of the employees and the aims and needs of the organization is self-defeating. One of the widely recognized needs for the years ahead is for a greater emphasis on innovation rather than on simply reacting to pressures, yet psychological research and theory indicate that innovation is much more likely to take place where individuals feel secure enough to take the risks involved, and where organizational reward systems encourage experimentation and exploration – which they have signally failed to do in the last decade. Seeking to help organizations realize the potential of their workforce in a mutually enhancing way is the business challenge psychology has to meet.

The aim of the *Essential Business Psychology* series is to interpret and explain people's work behaviour in the context of a continually evolving pattern of change, and to do so from the perspective of occupational and organizational psychology. The books draw together academic research and practitioner experience, relying on empirical studies, practical examples, and case studies to communicate their ideas. Hopefully, the reader will find that they provide a succinct summary of accumulated knowledge and how it can be applied. The themes of some of the books cover traditional areas of occupational psychology, while others will focus on topics that cut across some of these boundaries, tackling subjects that are of growing interest and prominence. The intended readership of the series is quite broad; whilst they are most directly relevant for practitioners, consultants, and students in HR and occupational psychology, much of what they deal with is increasingly the concern of managers and students of management more generally. Although the books share a common aim and series heading, they have not been forced into a rigid stylistic format. In keeping with the times, the authors have had a good deal of autonomy in deciding how to organize and present their work. I think all of them have done an excellent job; I hope you think so too.

Clive Fletcher

1 *Managing personnel selection for total quality*

INTRODUCTION

> The 1990s will be remembered by many organizations as their
> decade; many others won't be remembering it at all since they will
> have ceased to exist. The events of the 1990s will create such
> demands for change upon organizations that many will go under.
> The major reason they will do so is that they will fail to recruit and
> retain the people they need to help them change. People make the
> place, and people set the pace.
>
> (Herriot, 1989, p. 1).

Peter Herriot's forecast was timely and accurate. During the early
1990s changes were, as they still are, being forced on many
organizations by world-class competition, open markets, rising
customer expectations and demographic changes. In combination
these factors have converged to press many into optimizing their
competitive cost base via evaluations of organizational assets and
resources. After conducting these reviews many public- and private-
sector companies came to support Herriot's view of competitive
advantage residing in quality people, rather than other features. For
example, new product innovations produce only short-term advantages as competitors tend to quickly adopt and assimilate them into
their own products. Similarly, because corporate image is tempered
by customer experiences, it is not commercially viable to rely solely
on previous reputations. Continued organizational survival and
growth, therefore, depends on attracting and retaining high-calibre

people, while motivating them to apply their talents for the benefit of the organization.

The supply and demand of labour, however, is influenced by many factors, not least of which is the availability of suitably qualified employees. Employers' organizations have predicted serious short-falls in this respect for the mid-to-late 1990s. For example, the number of school leavers is estimated to fall by 1.3 million during this decade, resulting in intensive competition between traditional public-sector (e.g. police, health professions, military forces, etc.) and private-sector recruiters. Similarly, graduate recruitment will also be affected as women, mature graduates, ethnic minorities and disabled graduates compete with the traditional white, middle-class, 21-year-old male graduate for employment. In addition, current and projected skill shortages will compound the overall situation even further as the supply of the right people with the right skills becomes severely restricted. Inevitably, if organizations are not to be left behind, or go under, recruitment policies and selection procedures will have to be adapted to reflect the changing nature of the workforce.

Ironically, despite this backdrop of efficiency drives, increased competition and skill shortages, wasteful approaches to selection can be found in many organizations. For example, rather than working to ensure that selection procedures deliver the right people in the first place, many will let time decide whether decisions have been right or wrong. Often, selectors are unable or unwilling to spend time analysing the essential requirements of the job, and merely raise the qualification bar to simplify their task. However, this use of educational qualifications as a blanket measure of ability will not ensure the recruitment of the right people. At the present time, for example, it is not unusual to find 400 people with the right qualifications applying for a single vacancy. In these situations selection procedures can be little more than a lottery. Sometimes the organization wins, in that the person selected can do the job quite ably. Very often, however, the organization loses as the person either cannot do the job very well, or the job does not live up to expectations and he or she leaves soon after. Because personnel selection is concerned with predicting people's future behaviour on the job (always a difficult task), it is essential that the relevant abilities are properly assessed and measured so as to provide a sound basis for reflective decision-making. As Drucker (1986) states, 'what gets measured gets done'.

PSYCHOLOGY AND PERSONNEL SELECTION

Since the First World War psychologists have been studying and devising various methods of measuring human attributes with a view to predicting the future job performance of employees. The goal of these procedures is to identify potential and fit the right applicant to the job. By assessing the strengths and weaknesses of individuals, more is learnt about an applicant's abilities and aptitudes than is typically provided from educational qualifications and work experience information. Much of the research work in this area has focused upon the accuracy of psychological tests, interviews and other selection methods in predicting successful job performance, and has attempted to address the following two fundamental questions:

- How can selectors ensure that the candidates they choose are the ones who will perform better than rejected applicants?
- How can successful job performance be measured so that judgements can be made about the accuracy of selection decisions?

Not surprisingly, early evidence produced inconsistent results. In some studies, a particular selection method predicted subsequent job performance very well. In other studies the same selection method gave less impressive results. By the late 1970s the general conclusion was that methods may work well in some settings but not in others. This meant that it was thought necessary to carry out specific local validation studies each time a method was used in any new settings. During the 1980s, however, advances in statistical procedures forced researchers to reconsider this viewpoint, by showing that these inconsistent results were often due to the small samples of people typically used in the original validation studies. When the data from all of the available studies were combined to provide much larger sample sizes the results gave a more consistent picture. The results showed that for many of the major personnel selection methods, when there is good correspondence between the job and person specifications and the measuring instruments used, predictions are reasonably accurate. An example is provided by the construction division of the Trafalgar House Group, who adopted psychometric tests to select candidates for trainee management positions. They found, in comparison with previous trainee cohorts, the drop-out rate reduced significantly, while the success rate increased. What this means is that when selection methods are derived systematically to focus on the job in question, good results are obtained. This conclusion applies to many of the mainstream selection methods dealt with in later chapters of this book, but there are important exceptions.

In conjunction with these developments, recent advances in utility analysis have shown how the potential financial gains of good personnel selection can be estimated with some accuracy. For example, utility analyses indicated a net benefit of £800,000 to the police from using assessment centres to select senior police officers to attend a senior command course, when compared to the traditional rating system previously used. These developments have made it possible for personnel specialists to compete for organizational resources on equal terms with other managerial functions, such as marketing, finance, operations and accounting. Unfortunately, suc-cessive surveys regarding the use of selection methods indicate that most companies rely on the classic trio – application blanks, ad hoc interviews and reference checks – which are among the least reliable and valid selection methods. Although surveys also reveal clear moves by larger companies towards the use of assessment centres and psychometric testing, it appears that in many companies the choice of selection method(s) is more a function of expediency rather than technical adequacy. Thus, there is a noticeable gap between research findings and practical applications, even though it is possible to purchase psychological tests or contract the services of Chartered Occupational Psychologists to assist in the development of 'in-house' selection procedures.

Although there are clear gains to be had from the use of personnel selection methods some recent research has focused on the possible adverse effects of selection procedures on an individual's psychological well-being. It has become clear that candidates will express preferences for selection procedures that are clearly linked to the job in question. Considerable organizational benefits may be expected to flow from consideration of this issue. For example, procedures that incorporate work-sample tests not only provide candidates with the opportunity for self-assessment which subsequently tends to reduce employee turnover rates, but they also encourage highly motivated people to perform well while minimizing the possibility of adverse impact on minority groups. Conversely, selection procedures not thought by candidates to be closely linked to the job, tend to be disliked and perceived to be unfair. Similarly, unless care is taken over the assessment procedures used for internal promotions, the differing reactions of successful and rejected candidates may exert considerable influences on both the effectiveness of subsequent development programmes and people's intentions to quit jobs or careers. Potentially these issues can lead to very able people being lost to competitors as they self-select themselves out of either the selection process or the organization.

A related avenue of psychological research directly relevant to the changing nature of the workforce, is the perceived fairness of selection procedures. Companies that use selection procedures which discriminate against minority groups or discriminate on grounds of gender are likely to find themselves facing litigation suits from unsuccessful applicants. Unless there is clear evidence that selection procedures are both fair and highly related to successful job performance, companies will lose to litigants. The resulting fallout could be very serious. Compensation and legal costs, dents to corporate image, and a reluctance on the part of people to apply for future vacancies will all combine to weaken the organization's competitive edge seriously. Moreover, at the end of the day, the 'offending' selection procedures will have to be amended; this, perhaps more than any other reason, underscores the need for organizations to 'get it right first time'.

TOTAL QUALITY MANAGEMENT AND PERSONNEL SELECTION

Many organizations have been, or are responding to ever-increasing competitive pressures by actively embracing total quality management (TQM) techniques. In essence, these link product and service quality to customer satisfaction by institutionalizing continuous quality improvement, resulting in better long term business performance and profitability. In other words, where TQM initiatives have been or are being implemented, a positive corporate 'culture' change is continually taking place, the main focus of which is on providing quality products and services to customers. In 1991, Stephen Hill at the London School of Economics divided the concept of quality into two related aspects that are directly relevant to personnel selection. He placed particular emphasis upon the effectiveness of the product or service meeting the needs of the customer rather than the producer, by defining quality as 'conformance to the requirements of the customer', while also recognizing that the attainment of quality goals can be achieved only when the efficiency of operations within an organization are such that performance is fully optimized. Within this framework, the human resource (HR) function plays a crucial role in the attainment of quality goals by ensuring maximum efficiency of the organization's selection procedures to procure the best recruits available who conform to customer requirements. In the final analyses, the quality of these recruits will not only be reflected in the finished product or service provided by the organization, but will also reflect upon the quality and efficiency of the organization's selection process.

Failing to satisfy customer needs and expectations, or failing to 'get things right first time' has cost many a company dearly, with estimates suggesting costs somewhere between 10 and 30 per cent of sales revenue. Realizing that the control of quality costs can make a significant contribution to profitability, many companies have acknowledged that it is necessary to specify a 'framework for action' to guide continuous improvements. For most TQM initiatives this framework typically involves setting out an approach that

- identifies customer needs and expectations;
- sets quality standards that are consistent with customer requirements;
- controls and improves the capability of operational processes;
- specifies management's responsibility for setting quality goals, demonstrating leadership and providing the necessary resources;
- involves and empowers all employees to enact quality improvements.

Typically, the above 'framework for action' sets the scene for changing the culture of an organization as a whole. Very often, however, it is necessary to adapt this type of framework to the specific needs of each functional department to assist in the development of operational procedures which ensure that the quality of products or services are delivered 'right first time' at minimum cost.

Recruiting the right people first time round can result in considerable value being added to the employing organization. Some estimates suggest economic benefits equivalent to between 6 and 20 per cent of existing productivity levels. In some cases, particularly in small organizations, good personnel selection can be the difference between making a profit and sustaining a loss. Other organizational advantages may be gained from reduced absenteeism and employee turnover because of increased job satisfaction and organizational commitment resulting from a closer fitting of the person to the job. Nonetheless, selecting the right person for the job can be a difficult task because not all people or jobs are the same. People differ in size, intelligence, ability, personality and in their relative strengths and weaknesses while jobs differ in the demands they place on people in terms of their physical and mental workloads. These inherent differences often lead to selection decisions being made in the face of uncertainty. Accordingly, it makes good commercial sense to develop a specific 'framework for action' by setting out an approach to ensure a good match between a person's strengths, skills and abilities and the demands of the job he or she is required to do. A framework for systematic selection should specify the need to

- ensure that selectors have some understanding of how people differ in different situations;
- identify customers' needs and expectations via job analyses;
- set standards that meet customer requirements;
- establish evaluative standards with which to assess the selection method(s) used;
- set evaluative standards to assess the efficiency of the selection procedure(s);
- identify the most appropriate selection method(s) for the job(s) in question;
- set decision-making standards;
- develop further ideas for continuous improvement.

The benefits to be gained from this type of framework reside in the systematic assessment and matching of individual recruits to specific job demands, while also providing the means to monitor and assess the efficiency of the selection system *per se*. Within the context of this framework the 'customer' is usually internal to the organization: for example, the head of a functional department or project management team. In some instances, particularly in smaller organizations, it is recognized that the owner or director may be both 'customer' and 'supplier' in that he or she may conduct the recruitment and selection procedures themselves. Nonetheless, throughout the remainder of the book we refer to 'customer(s)' as the person(s), department(s), or organization(s) that instigated the requirement for new recruits.

The above 'framework for action' provides the focus for this book, beginning with Chapter 2 which centres on individual differences. As it is not uncommon to find line management, or other non-HR specialists involved in the selection of people, it is particularly important that they have an appreciation of people factors. Thus, this chapter aims to provide some understanding of the ways in which personal factors and situational demands interact to influence people's behaviour on the job. For example, the performance of salespeople will be influenced by their personality and ability as well as the geographical area in which they must operate. Assessing person and job factors within this context clarifies, directs and optimizes the overall process of identifying customer needs, as well as guiding choices of appropriate selection methods and ultimately the candidates themselves.

Chapter 3 concentrates on methodologies to identify customers needs and set the requisite standards. It is often the case, for example, that a departmental manager will ask for a vacant position to be filled in the expectation that the personnel office already knows what is required of the job and the job holder. In some instances this may be true, but typically this is not so, as many job requirements change over a period of time. Consequently, in the same way that many workplace initiatives require careful forethought and preparation if mistakes and hitches are to be avoided, it makes sense to identify systematically the salient features of the job and the personal characteristics required of the job holder. Job analysis is the generic term used to describe methodologies that allow personnel specialists to set the necessary standards by discovering exactly what the job entails and which skills and abilities are necessary for successful job performance. Hence, job analyses simultaneously satisfy three goals by:

- identifying the specific characteristics of people who are best equipped to meet the demands of the job;
- identifying the criteria by which a candidate's work performance will be assessed;
- setting appropriate evaluative standards.

Once the analysis has been completed the personnel specialist should be able to develop clearly written personnel specifications and job descriptions that specify the minimum standards required. Without either one of these formal documents, systematic selection becomes impossible. These standards are the benchmarks by which any subsequent processes that make up the selection procedure are assessed.

Chapter 4 is concerned with establishing the necessary standards of the selection method(s) themselves to ensure that the basis for decision-making is optimized. If quality standards are to be achieved, the measurement of quality attributes to provide performance feedback is a vital if somewhat troublesome aspect of quality management systems. Equally, if prospective candidates are to meet the standards derived from job analysis, a difficult but vital feature of a personnel selection system is the measurement of psychological attributes and job-related behaviours. In both cases the challenge resides in the need for measurement systems to be

- reliable;
- accurate;
- interpretable;
- practical.

Each of these four attributes is an evaluative standard by which the quality of a measurement system should be assessed. Failing to meet any one of them will lead to faulty measurement and poor decision-making that might cause significant costs to be incurred.

Chapter 5 focuses on the evaluative standards with which to assess the overall selection procedure(s) so that errors in design and implementation can be identified and assessed. Because TQM systems are designed and implemented according to established written standards so that deviations can be recognized and corrected, the same must apply to selection procedures if their quality is to be assured. A design-cycle technology is described that optimizes return on investment by providing a systematic framework within which evaluations of the system's quality can be made. The main standards that apply are effectiveness, efficiency and fairness, which are assessed respectively in terms of information yield, benefit/cost ratios and adverse impact. Failure to identify errors in any one of these areas may lead to unsuitable candidates being selected at vast cost, while landing the organization in court for discriminating against minority groups.

Chapters 6 to 9 concentrate on the wide range of selection

methods that are currently available so that selectors are better informed as to their usefulness. This should assist selectors to choose the most appropriate methods, according to the particular circumstances. Within each of these chapters the evaluative standards of the various selection methods are also discussed. Chapter 6 is concerned purely with selection interviewing in its different forms, as often this is the sole means used for selecting people. Chapter 7 is concerned with a variety of sample based selection methods, and includes various types of work-sample tests and exercises commonly used in assessment centres. Chapter 8 focuses on the use of psychometric instruments to measure individual differences and covers cognitive and personality testing, biographical data and honesty testing. Chapter 9 focuses on alternative selection methods that are available, some more useful than others; it includes references, educational qualifications, self- and peer assessments, graphology and astrology.

Chapter 10 is concerned with setting decision-making standards to ensure the right candidates are chosen. In general, there are two types of decision-making: statistical and judgemental. To control operational processes most types of TQM initiatives follow the statistical method with techniques such as Pareto analysis, statistical process control (SPC), process flow charting, scatter diagrams etc. Personnel selection decision-making, however, is almost always based on the selector's judgements. As would be expected, considerable evidence shows the statistical method to be better than selectors' judgements. Various statistical methods are available to aid selectors in their decision-making and are more in accordance with the requirements of a quality personnel selection procedure. The advantages of the statistical approach not only reside in the fact that the better applicants are more likely to be chosen, but year on year a database can be compiled to aid in the validation of an organization's selection methods and procedures. The quality of applicants can be monitored on a yearly basis, and it is possible to identify those operational areas with a large turnover of employees, which may indicate areas of operational concern. The ethnic and gender make-up of applicants can also be monitored, and this may help to avoid any unintentional unfair discrimination. The statistical methods outlined in Chapter 10 help to provide a series of feedback loops to the human resource department, these will help to optimize an organization's selection procedures and return on investment.

Chapter 11 highlights emerging trends, issues and challenges in the field of personnel selection, and includes the use of computer based assessments, ethical and research issues.

SUMMARY

In today's highly competitive climate, organizational survival and growth are dependent upon attracting, recruiting and retaining quality people. Because personnel specialists are the guardians of key organizational processes such as selection, appraisal, training and reward systems which link corporate policies with action, they exert a considerable influence on the outcomes of quality management initiatives. For example, if unsuitable people are employed, the quality of the organization's products or services will inevitably suffer. This may cause further losses associated with quality, productivity, reliability and corporate image. In turn, this may lead to shrinkages in the organization's client base which ultimately may cause the demise of the organization. Because of the changing nature of the workforce and increasing shortages of skilled people it is crucial that personnel specialists apply quality principles to their own activities to ensure they get it right first time. This book offers a 'framework for action' within which the human resource function or line managers can apply TQM principles to personnel selection to assist in the optimization of an organization's selection procedures.

2 How people differ

People are different. In fact one of the most remarkable things about human beings is that no two are the same. Even twins with identical genetic material (monozygotic twins) develop into unique individuals with their own interests and personalities. At a superficial, physical level, differences between people are obvious and most of us could list some of the major ways in which people differ physically: height, weight and colouring, for example. Some physical characteristics are less obvious and it may be necessary to collect a sample of behaviour or to conduct some measurements to establish an individual's position. As far as psychological characteristics are concerned there is nothing that is as obvious as a person's height or weight. Indeed to understand anything at all about an individual's psychological make-up requires that some kind of detailed observation be undertaken. Both the major dimensions on which we differ and the reliable measurement of individuals, in relation to these dimensions, have been the subject of specialized research by psychologists. This work and its relevance to personnel selection provide the focus for this chapter.

The case of Bobby Taylor provides a good example of the importance of psychological characteristics in the workplace. Bobby developed a keen interest in football during his teenage years and represented his county at schoolboy level. Upon leaving school he joined his local club as a trainee professional. Bobby's unpredictable and vigorous attacking style brought him goals at youth-team, reserves and, by the age of 18, first-team level. Midway through his second season in the first team one of the big clubs made a successful bid for Bobby and he moved on to play for them. Several more successful seasons followed and Bobby was among the top few goalscorers in the league every season. He represented his country several times but was never able to establish himself as a natural first choice. The press and TV pundits often made claims that his skilful and excitable style should have been developed more effectively within the framework of the national team. These claims were rarely supported by Bobby's international colleagues even though they described him as a friendly and agreeable team mate who tried very hard to fit in and do a good job.

When he was 28 and again on the verge of making a major impact at international level Bobby sustained a minor injury which meant that he could not play for a while. Bobby was very keen to be selected to play for his country in a forthcoming World Cup match, and persuaded his club manager to allow him to begin playing again, before his injury was fully healed. In his first game after returning from injury Bobby was anxious to prove to the watching international manager that he was match-fit and in good form. Unfortunately, early in the game Bobby stretched to make a difficult interception at the same time as he was tackled by an opposing player. He never recovered fully from the resulting injury and gave up playing two years later.

After retiring as a player Bobby worked in partnership with some other sporting personalities in a sports goods company. Bobby was very successful on the sales side. He was extremely conscientious and while his colleagues focused on product development and made ambitious plans for the company's future Bobby's drive and agreeable personality ensured a steady stream of orders. The company flourished and with his earnings as a player and the income from the company Bobby soon became financially secure. Although Bobby enjoyed his work he had little interest in the commercial side of things and spent a lot of his time in football-related activities. He became involved in coaching, on a part-time basis at first, but gradually this grew to the point when he sold his share in the sports goods company, so that he could become a full-time coach with a top-class club. A couple of years after Bobby had taken up his coaching position the manager of the club resigned unexpectedly to take a job abroad and Bobby was offered the job. He had been a very popular and successful coach and few people were surprised that he was given the opportunity of taking the manager's job.

Initially results went well but after injuries to some of the key players forced a change of tactics on Bobby the side began to lose games and slide down the league table. At the end of Bobby's first season they narrowly avoided relegation and it was clear that a good start to the new season was important if Bobby was to retain his job. In fact, things went from bad to worse when the new season started. Bobby seemed unable to find a settled team and changed players from week to week. He also experimented with new tactical formations. As matters got worse, Bobby became increasingly tense and irritable and began to be away from the club a great deal, leaving crucial decisions to others. Eventually he was fired.

 What this example shows clearly is that psychological characteristics that are well matched to one role may not always be functional in another setting. In Bobby Taylor's case his footballing skills brought success on the field. Like many people who achieve outstanding success Bobby had a great deal of drive, triggered, in part, by an anxiety to do well and avoid failure. This will have provided the motivation to practise and struggle for success. His career as a player almost certainly benefited from his tense, anxious disposition. On the other hand his lack of recognition at international level was probably due to high drive and anxiety leading him to overextend himself and perform erratically. His highly anxious and striving personality also clearly contributed to his career-ending injury. His commercial career flourished on the basis of his tendency to be concerned about doing things well (i.e. conscientiousness) and his agreeable personal style. For people with high levels of anxiety, like Bobby, operating in challenging circumstances can be a problem and often their decision-making skills break down. In the sports goods company there were few times when things were difficult, and in any case Bobby's colleagues concentrated their energies on the commercial aspects of the business, leaving Bobby relatively free of stress. As a coach Bobby was again relatively free from stressful demands. He did not have responsibility for selecting the team, which in any case did well under the existing manager. He did not have to buy or sell players, nor was there any general tension at the club while things were going well. Taking on the manager's role exposed Bobby to a set of circumstances that he was not equipped to deal with.

INDIVIDUAL DIFFERENCES

With physical characteristics the most common and obvious ways in which we differ are well known and we all share a common framework for viewing others. For more complex physiological factors the dimensions of difference and their measurement are less immediately apparent and require more specialized knowledge to assess. Factors such as cholesterol level, lung capacity, visual acuity and aspects of fitness or strength are reasonably well-known dimensions of difference. Most people have some grasp of the existence of these kinds of differences and an appreciation of their importance but could not make accurate assessments of them. In very general terms psychologists divide human psychological character-istics into two broad categories: personality and cognitive abilities. Cognitive ability concerns people's capacity to process verbal, numerical and other kinds of information. Personality refers to individual differences in temperament or disposition.

Cognitive ability

As far as cognitive ability is concerned there is a well-established framework which can be used to describe people. At the most general level in this framework there is general intelligence or g, sometimes referred to as general mental ability. The usefulness of general intelligence as a concept was established many years ago when researchers were interested in describing human intellectual capabil-ities. It became clear in the first part of this century that, when scores on a range of different intellectual tasks were considered, people who did well on one type of task (e.g. one involving words) also tended to do well on other tasks even if they were apparently rather different (e.g. using numbers or shapes). In other words there seemed to be some general capacity to process information that was not entirely specific to the kind of information being dealt with. It was also clear, however, that, up to a point, people did exhibit different strengths and weaknesses in processing various kinds of information; so some people did relatively well on say, numerical data, whereas others did their best with verbal material.

The underlying theory to explain these results was originally put forward by Burt (1940) and developed by Vernon (1961). This theory provides a role for both general mental ability and specific factors (see Figure 2.1). These kinds of research results led Spearman to propose the two factor theory of the structure of intelligence (Spearman, 1927). Essentially this theory proposed that there is a general intelligence factor (g) plus a range of specific factors(s) which, when taken together, explain people's overall information-processing capacity and their differential aptitudes in various specific areas. General intelligence (g) is responsible for the correlation which exists between performance of different types of task, while more specific abilities explain the fact that no one performs equally well or badly on everything. General intelligence sits at the top of a hierarchy which also includes various levels of specific factors. Performance on mental (cognitive) tasks is determined by a combination of g and underlying factors. This structure for human cognitive ability has proved very resilient and still provides a base for the work of many applied psychologists, including most who work in the personnel selection field.

There are other approaches to human intellectual functioning. One of the most influential alternative approaches stresses that to function intelligently in everyday life one needs to grapple successfully with problems that are very different from the relatively clear-cut and purely cognitive questions that make up a typical intelligence test. Sternberg and others (see Sternberg and Wagner, 1986) use the term 'practical intelligence' to refer to the kind of thinking that is needed to function on a day-to-day basis. Organizing a social or working event, choosing the best buy from a range of products, or planning a journey are all examples of activities that require intelligent behaviour. The behaviour called for is highly varied and interlinked with social and emotional factors. One of the key features of practical thinking is that it is embedded in everyday experience and is instrumental in solving real-world problems (Scribner, 1986). This is in direct contrast to the abstract and isolated nature of the kind of

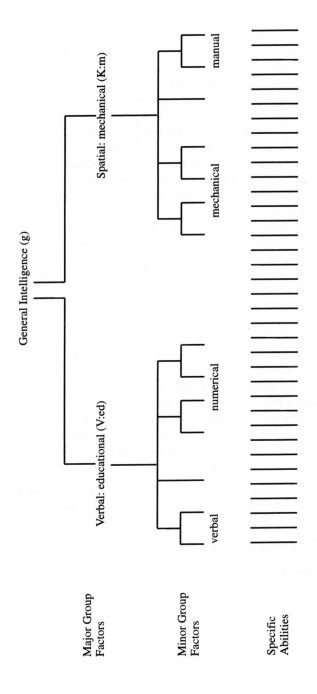

Major Group Factors

Minor Group Factors

Specific Abilities

General Intelligence (g)

Verbal: educational (V:ed)

Spatial: mechanical (K:m)

verbal

numerical

mechanical

manual

Figure 2.1 Vernon's model of the structure of intelligence
Source: Based on Vernon (1961)

problems included in typical intelligence tests (see Figure 2.2). Advocates of practical intelligence argue that there are crucial features in the kind of thinking that is required in real life that cannot be captured in written tests. There is almost certainly some validity in this view but it is important to note that there are strong relationships between scores on psychometric tests of cognitive ability and various aspects of everyday behaviour. In the work domain, for example, there is a long and convincing stream of research evidence to show that scores on mental ability tests are correlated well with indicators of overall work proficiency in very many occupational areas. This research is covered more fully in Chapter 8.

The existence of standardized psychometric tests for g and underlying sub-factors such as spatial, numerical or verbal ability is one of the main advantages that the traditional approach to the structure of human cognitive abilities has. These standardized tests provide a basis for assessing people's cognitive abilities and, as already noted, strong links exist between scores on these tests and measures of work behaviour. Tests exist for both g and most of the sub-factors. In the UK there are several specialist companies that publish psychological tests and most of them have a reasonably wide range of tests. In other words, there is not just one test available for each aspect of cognitive ability. In fact, developing, publishing and marketing psychological tests has become a sizeable commercial activity. Most of the companies that produce psychological tests also offer other services, including training and consultancy provided by highly qualified Chartered Occupational Psychologists. The provi-

PRACTICAL INTELLIGENCE	INTELLIGENCE TESTS
• Giving change to a customer	• Arithmetic operations
• Assembling components	• Identifying next shape in series
• Taking an inventory	• Matching similar words

Figure 2.2 Practical intelligence vs intelligence tests

sion of services by Chartered Occupational Psychologists in the UK is monitored by the British Psychological Society (BPS) and there is a professional code of conduct that Chartered Psychologists must follow. Most test publishers provide training in line with BPS recommendations and it is possible for non-psychologists to become qualified in the use and interpretation of some psychological tests.

People, situations and behaviour

People differ significantly from one another in terms of cognitive ability and often these differences serve to act as defining features of an individual; someone who is particularly able with numerical material may, even at a fairly early age, be distinguished from others on this basis. If asked to describe the distinguishing features of friends or acquaintances, however, most of us would not focus for long on intellectual qualities. Think of how you would describe close friends or people in your immediate family; most of the descriptive terms that you might use will refer to personal qualities such as each person's tendency to be reliable, sociable, irritable and so on. Two things are interesting to note here. The first point is that we will commonly describe others as if they have stable personal characteristics that are consistent from one time and place to another. The second is that these personal characteristics are related to aspects of disposition or temperament much more than to intellectual qualities. It may seem obvious that people have stable personal qualities that influence how they behave in various different situations but the degree of influence exerted by these qualities on behaviour is not at all clear, even after only a moment or two of reflection. Consider for instance someone's behaviour in a selection interview. Even someone who is quite dominant and extroverted in other settings, will probably defer to the interviewer and allow him or her to set the agenda for discussion. By contrast, the interviewee will be very forceful and dominant in a meeting at work with a group of peers. Which behaviour represents the real person? Is our behaviour due to the situation (e.g. being in an interview rather than being at a party) or is it caused by underlying, stable personal qualities?

These kinds of questions have been of great interest to psychologists for many years. Research has shown that the answer to the puzzle of whether the person or the situation causes behaviour is that both are fundamentally important. In fact our behaviour interacts in a complex way with internal psychological characteristics and situational factors. The diagram in Figure 2.3 gives some indication of how behavioural, personal and situational factors all interact. As the figure suggests, the situations that surround us are partly the product of our own behaviour. In extreme cases we can remove ourselves from some situations entirely, or we may take some action that will have an impact on the situation: for example, we can walk away from an angry disagreement between two colleagues or we may intervene. Different behaviour on our part will have different influences on the situation.

It is important to recognize that, more often than not, the most salient features of any situation are the other people who are present. Whether or not someone intervenes in a disagreement between others will depend on many factors but will certainly be dependent, to a degree, on his or her own personality. In turn the development of each individual's personality is partly determined by the situations that he or she has been exposed to in the past. So, as Figure 2.3 shows, personal qualities, situations and behaviour are continuously interacting with each other. This view of human psychological mechanisms is based on the work of the American psychologist, Albert Bandura (Bandura, 1986) and is known as 'reciprocal determinism'. According to this view the question of whether it is personal qualities or situations that determine behaviour makes no sense; people's psychological qualities and the situation they are in interact to influence behaviour. In turn, behaviour may work to exert effects on people or situations.

There is quite a lot of research evidence which demonstrates these interacting effects. In one particularly well-designed piece of work the investigators (Kohn and Schooler, 1982) collected evidence on how job characteristics and personal qualities interacted. In a longitudinal study which involved data from several time points they found that people who were intellectually flexible (i.e. able to see problems from different perspectives) tended to be attracted to jobs that required intellectual flexibility. Over time, because of the demands of their work the intellectual flexibility of these people grew and led them to seek out positions that required higher levels of intellectual flexibility. This is a clear demonstration of how personal qualities help to determine the situations that people are exposed to and how, in turn, these situations influence personal qualities.

It should be clear from the above that even with a very good knowledge of someone's cognitive ability and personality it would

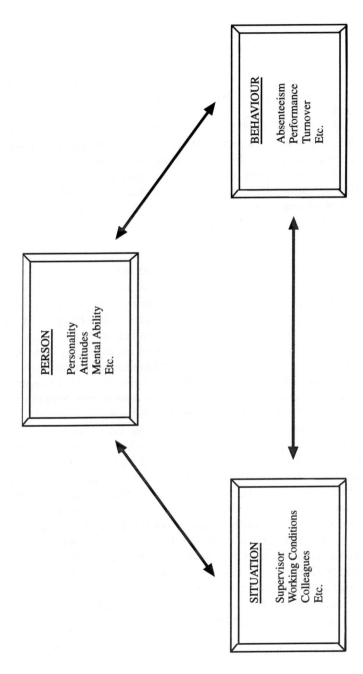

Figure 2.3 Interactions between person, situation and behaviour

The boxes in the figure contain:

BEHAVIOUR

Absenteeism
Performance
Turnover
Etc.

PERSON

Personality
Attitudes
Mental Ability
Etc.

SITUATION

Supervisor
Working Conditions
Colleagues
Etc.

be impossible to predict behaviour with complete certainty because situational factors will also be important. Some people who seem well suited to a particular position fail to be successful because of situational factors, such as the influence of other people or external events. Bobby Taylor was successful in one setting but not in another.

Although a knowledge of someone's personality and cognitive ability cannot give a perfect picture of how someone will behave it is possible to predict future behaviour with some degree of success, especially if some key aspects of the situation are understood (e.g. the kind of job involved). The use of personality and ability testing in personnel selection is covered in more detail in Chapter 8 and job analysis is covered in Chapter 3.

Personality

Whereas cognitive ability is concerned with people's capacity to process information, personality is more to do with people's style of behaviour. Differences in temperament or disposition form the core of what is generally referred to as personality. Historically there has been some dispute amongst psychologists about the very existence of stable individual differences in personality. This debate was fuelled by the fact that people often behaved inconsistently from one situation to another. Some psychologists took this to imply that situations were largely responsible for determining behaviour and that the role of stable individual differences was minimal. This debate becomes redundant if one takes the kind of position outlined in the previous section of this chapter where person, situation and behavioural variables are constantly interacting. This interactional view also emphasizes the point that perfectly accurate predictions about behaviour are impossible, with our current state of knowledge, given the complex interplay of the forces involved. More certain predictions are possible when one of the forces involved is likely to be dominant. It is not difficult, for example, to predict that under normal circumstances most people will talk very little when the main film is showing in a cinema. This is an example of a very strong situation exerting an influence. When the situational influences are weaker, such as in a casual gathering of people at a social event, it is quite likely that gregarious outgoing individuals will talk a fair bit!

The hierarchical structure of intelligence outlined in Figure 2.1

gives a clear, reasonably well accepted picture of human cognitive abilities. Until quite recently the structure of personality was much less clear and many different theoretical perspectives were in existence. During the last ten years or so a clear five-dimension framework for the structure of personality has emerged. This structure, the 'Big Five' is the product of an intensive stream of research that has been under way for more than half a century. As long ago as the 1940s Hans Eysenck identified two of the main dimensions of human personality: Extroversion and Neuroticism (anxiety). According to Eysenck the typical extrovert 'is sociable, likes parties, has many friends to talk to and does not like reading or studying [alone]'. Extroverts also enjoy excitement, practical jokes and change, in addition to exhibiting aggressive and impulsive tendencies. The typical neurotic generally experiences feelings of tension and anxiety, with a tendency to worry a great deal and be emotionally unstable. As noted in the case study, Bobby Taylor's high level of anxiety contributed to his success and to his failure. These two features of personality are independent of one another (i.e. a person's position on one conveys no information about his or her position on the other) and four major personality types may be identified: unstable (neurotic) extrovert, unstable introvert, stable extrovert and stable introvert.

A very substantial amount of research has confirmed the prominence of these factors in determining behaviour. It is worth stressing again that personality differences such as these are only partly responsible for determining behaviour. Even quite withdrawn, introverted people can be outgoing in some situations and people who are generally anxious find relaxation in some settings. The crucial point is that personality differences predispose people to behave in certain ways but these predispositions are tempered by situational influences.

Although extroversion and emotional stability have been part of most personality psychologists' frameworks for some time, the other dimensions in the Big Five have become universally accepted more recently. In addition to extroversion and emotional stability the other dimensions in the Big Five are: *Agreeableness*, a tendency to be good-natured and compassionate, warm with other people and to seek to avoid conflict; *Conscientiousness*, a predisposition to be well organized, concerned about meeting goals and deadlines, and making and implementing plans; *Openness to Experience*, a propensity to be imaginative, flexible with broad interests and hold a positive, open-minded view of new experiences (see Costa and McCrae, 1985).

The Big Five
- Extroversion–Introversion
- Emotional Stability
- Agreeableness
- Conscientiousness
- Openness to Experience

The existence of the Big Five provides a useful organizing framework at a fairly high level of generality but it does not make the use of other personality dimensions pointless. Sometimes it is productive to gain a more detailed picture of an individual's personality and far more dimensions than five are then needed. Even personality inventories based specifically on the Big Five provide measurement of many underlying dimensions. Examples of more detailed personality characteristics measured by various inventories include: group dependence, detail consciousness, social confidence, dominance and proneness to 'feeling' guilt.

Personality inventories and measures of cognitive ability are, however, costly and time-consuming to develop and their construction is a job for specialists. The construction and evaluation of these measures is briefly described in Chapter 4 and their use in personnel selection is discussed in Chapter 8.

Personal competencies

Instead of concentrating on underlying differences in cognition or temperament that might be related to work performance the investigation of personal competencies seeks to look directly at key performance-related factors. Competencies are relatively new terms for many human resource practitioners. To psychologists they are also new but seem, in many ways, to be no more than a different way of labelling concepts that have been useful for a long period. For decades psychologists and some human resource professionals have used terms such as knowledge, skills and abilities to represent the factors that underlie the effective performance of tasks.

The popularity of the idea of competencies in organizations has had the very positive effect of directing people's attention towards the skills and abilities of the workforce rather than other personal qualities (e.g. years of experience, qualifications) that are not necessarily as closely related to performance. A widely known book by Boyatzis (*The Competent Manager*, 1982) is usually credited with stimulating the recent interest in competencies in personnel and human resources practice. The adoption of competency-based approaches in organizations has been widespread and there is little doubt that it has had a beneficial effect on many aspects of organizational life. As Boam and Sparrow (1992) put it, such approaches can provide 'the glue to integrate recruitment, reward and development strategies ... [and provide] ... a focal point for change' (p. 175).

GENERIC COMPETENCIES

Different jobs and families of jobs will obviously require different mixtures of competencies and in any single organization a wide range of different competencies will be needed; nevertheless it is possible that some universally applicable common set of competencies might be able to be identified in the same way that the Big Five dimensions can be used as a framework for differences in personality. Any such generic set of competencies would have obvious appeal and value. The overall benefit of the approach in recruitment, development and other human resource activities (transferable competencies and a common language to describe them) would be significantly enhanced. Because of the attraction of this goal it is not surprising that several different generic frameworks have emerged (the very fact that this can happen suggests that the long-term stability of the current systems may be uncertain).

One of the best-known systems has been developed by Management Charter Initiative (1990). Other sets of generic competencies exist. Dulewicz (1989), for example, has devoted attention to the competencies needed at middle-management level and produced a set of generic 'supra-competencies' in four major categories: intellectual, interpersonal, adaptability and results orientation (see Table 2.1). Those responsible for human resources in many organizations have conducted work to identify the competencies that they feel are important for successful performance in that organization. Many of the competencies identified for this reason do look rather similar to those put forward by Dulewicz (1989) and others. This is taken by some to support the notion that a generic set of competencies is feasible but it could merely be the result of a common set of

Table 2.1 Dulewicz's supra-competencies

Intellectual	Strategic perspective
	Analysis and judgement
	Planning and organizing
Interpersonal	Managing staff
	Persuasiveness
	Assertiveness and decisiveness
	Interpersonal sensitivity
	Oral communication
Adaptability	Adaptability and resilience
Results orientation	Energy and initiative
	Achievement motivation
	Business sense

Source: Dulewicz (1989).

assumptions amongst the investigators, coupled with the use of similar terminology.

The idea that work competencies can be identified and measured with accuracy is taken for granted when, in fact, it is an assumption worth questioning. The first issue worthy of critical inspection is the concept of competency itself. Many authors write in a very 'matter of fact' way about competencies, stating that they are concerned with behaviour and sometimes defining competencies as dimensions of overt behaviour. Even a cursory glance at the lists of competencies referred to above shows that they are not behaviours. Behaviour needs to be defined unambiguously and it must be observable. Most of the commonly used competencies are not sufficiently specific or observable to be classified as behaviours.

There is no commonly accepted definition of a competency and almost all of the competencies given in typical generic or organization-specific systems are capable of being interpreted in several different ways and are not linked unambiguously to specific acts. Even the more thoughtful writers who deal with competencies seem to be uncertain about whether they are dealing with behaviour, predispositions to behave, skills, knowledge or some combination of many of these concepts. This uncertainty makes the measurement of people's competencies a challenging endeavour. As such the measurement of competencies is the second issue worthy of critical evaluation. Although many generic and specific competency frameworks exist, very few provide complementary evidence that the competencies in the framework can be defined clearly, that the different competencies are distinctive rather than overlapping, and that they can be measured with accuracy. The evidence that is available suggests that the identification, definition and, most importantly, measurement of independent, work-related competencies is, at the moment, beyond the skills of most practitioners.

One fairly common organizational event that involves the measurement of competencies is the use of assessment centres. Recent years have seen an increase in the use of assessment centres for personnel selection, promotion or development purposes. There is no doubt that assessment centre scores are correlated reasonably well with indicators of subsequent work success (Gaugler et al., 1987). In other words the criterion-related validity (see Chapter 7) of assessment centres is good. Assessment centres involve trained assessors observing candidates on a series of exercises (e.g. group discussions, in-trays, presentations, role plays) and assessing the candidates' performance on a set of competencies (sometimes referred to as 'dimensions' or 'attributes'). Problems arise when the assessment of candidates' performance, on the competencies, is looked at critically. There is clear evidence that the more competencies that are included in assessment centres the less accurate the assessors' judgements become (Gaugler and Thornton, 1989); this is perhaps not unexpected and could be remedied by using fewer dimensions. More troubling is evidence that the assessors' judgements of candidates' competencies will vary, depending on which exercise the candidate is conducting. Obviously some degree of variation in performance might be expected, from one exercise to another, and observing candidates on several exercises (i.e. in several different situations) should even things out and provide a more reliable view of candidates' competencies. The problem lies in the finding (see Chapter 7) that the assessors' scores reflect the different exercises much more than they reflect the different competencies. This is a serious problem because it means that competencies are not generalizable attributes that remain stable across different settings. The implication of this is that either there is something wrong with the measurement procedures or there is something wrong with the principle of transferable competencies.

SUMMARY

This chapter has identified the major categories of human individual differences: personality characteristics and cognitive abilities. The structure of cognitive abilities involves both a general intelligence (g) factor and more specific abilities. As far as personality is concerned the emergence of the Big Five (Extroversion, Emotional Stability, Conscientiousness, Agreeableness and Openness to Experience) has provided a clear framework for looking at individual differences in disposition. For occupational purposes it is often useful to look at individual differences in personal competencies. Various frameworks for work-related personal competencies exist but there are unresolved problems concerning the nature and measurement of such competencies.

3 Identifying customer needs and setting the required standards

Although it had a good share of the market and a popular product line, the 'Komet motorcycle company' was being hampered by ageing inner-city premises, and decided to move to a new purpose-built factory with the latest technology in a new developing town, approximately 100 miles away. Some of the existing employees had decided to move with the company, but many others were taking the enhanced redundancy package on offer. A different motorcycle company, 'Stallion', was also moving from inner-city premises to a greenfield site, and as for its competitor, some staff had decided to move with the company, but many had not. This meant that both companies needed to recruit many new staff for a variety of jobs.

Six months prior to the move, the Komet company management decided that in their new premises, they wanted to recruit people into workgroups rather than into specific jobs. Therefore each new employee had to be capable of performing all the jobs within a workgroup. The personnel manager was given the task of drafting employee and job specifications for each group of jobs, to use for selection purposes. The Stallion company management found that most of the people who were taking redundancy were shopfloor employees such as assemblers, mechanics, forklift drivers, packers and welders. Although these jobs were fairly skilled, requiring some experience and qualifications, while the remainder were semi-skilled or unskilled jobs, they felt that they could simply advertise all of the posts in the local paper, and fill the vacancies for each of these positions.

The Komet company's personnel team used a variety of data-gathering methods. First, they observed and questioned experienced job holders. Next they analysed all of the current jobs using the Job Components Inventory (Banks et al., 1983). This method is good for identifying in great detail the kinds of tools being used, the levels of mathematical reasoning, etc., involved in a job. It is also not necessary for job holders to be able to use complex vocabulary. In addition, the Position Analysis Questionnaire (McCormick et al., 1972) was used to identify the importance of each job, in relation to other jobs, in terms of the skill, effort and other demands made on job holders. This allowed different groups of jobs to be identified in a meaningful way. Those jobs identified as complex were subjected to further analysis using the Critical Incidents Technique (Flanagan, 1954), with supervisors providing descriptions of real job behaviour which they had witnessed, and rating these behaviours as effective or ineffective. The results of each type of analysis were combined to produce five distinct groupings of jobs. For each grouping of jobs a person specification was developed, along with the specific skills and abilities required for each group of jobs. For each of the skills identified, an interview checklist was devised, with guidelines on the type of questions to ask and information on how to interpret applicants' responses (see Chapter 6). The appropriate psychometric tests for each group of jobs were also identified (see Chapter 8).

On the basis of this procedure, the Komet company recruited its new workforce, which was subsequently found to be of a much higher quality than the previous workforce. For example, it was found that the normal training time for the new job holders decreased from an average of twelve weeks to six, and that there was very little turnover of new employees. Con-

> versely, the Stallion company, which had simply relied on trade qualifications or previous work experience found a high turnover of new employees, and that the training of new employees was still in the region of twelve weeks.

The above example is based on an actual study (Kandola, 1989), and provides a gross illustration of the way in which effective job analyses can aid an organization in its selection procedures. By identifying and focusing on the elements of a job that are crucial to good performance, the Komet company was able to derive job and person specifications by which important candidate attributes could be established. In contrast, the Stallion company did not undertake this process and subsequently found little difference in the quality of its workforce, training times or performance. The Komet example also shows that the first stage of filling a vacancy, that of undertaking job analyses, can be completed long before a vacancy actually arises. Figure 3.1 details the factors typically considered when a thorough job analysis is used to identify customer needs.

IDENTIFYING CUSTOMER NEEDS VIA JOB ANALYSES

Selection concerns are often not the sole reason for undertaking job analyses. They can be used for a variety of purposes such as identifying training needs, determining the health and safety aspects of jobs, producing a more rational and acceptable salary structure, annual staff performance appraisals, and reorganizing the company workforce. These examples are not the definitive list of uses. Levine (1983) mentions eleven uses. Because there are so many purposes, a great number of job analysis methods are available. They vary according to the type of job data, the method of data collection, the information sources and the methods of data analysis. The range of possible uses is so large that Brinkman (1983) devised a classification scheme for job analysis methods, making it possible to compare the utility (see Chapter 5) of different methods for specific organizational purposes. The method(s) finally chosen will obviously depend upon the exact situation and the intended use, although, in situations where limited resources are the norm and the consequences of a poor appointment are not too great, a simple approach is more likely to be

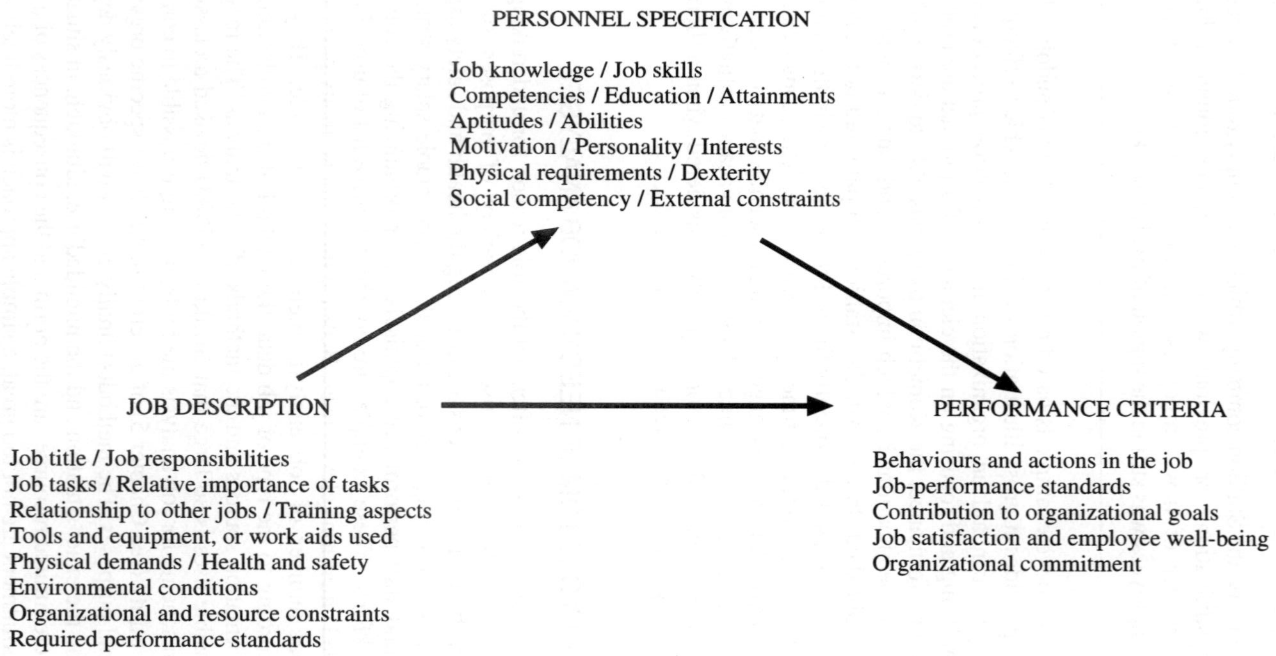

PERSONNEL SPECIFICATION

Job knowledge / Job skills
Competencies / Education / Attainments
Aptitudes / Abilities
Motivation / Personality / Interests
Physical requirements / Dexterity
Social competency / External constraints

PERFORMANCE CRITERIA

Behaviours and actions in the job
Job-performance standards
Contribution to organizational goals
Job satisfaction and employee well-being
Organizational commitment

JOB DESCRIPTION

Job title / Job responsibilities
Job tasks / Relative importance of tasks
Relationship to other jobs / Training aspects
Tools and equipment, or work aids used
Physical demands / Health and safety
Environmental conditions
Organizational and resource constraints
Required performance standards

Figure 3.1 Job-analysis factors to identify customer needs

adopted. In these instances it is likely that a straightforward analysis of jobs along six or seven major dimensions will suffice. In large organizations, where hundreds of recruits are sought each year, such as the military, telecommunications and banking, it is worth undertaking rigorous job analyses as the consequences of selection mistakes can be very costly to the organization. For example, employing an unsuitable candidate in a control room of a nuclear power station could, in an emergency, result in millions of pounds worth of damage and considerable pollution of the local environment. Similarly, recruiting and training a policeman can cost over £100,000. If recruits leave when their training is complete, or are deemed to be unsuitable during the training period, the organization will bear the brunt of these costs in addition to those of finding and training a replacement.

Different approaches to job analyses

One of the most comprehensive lists of techniques for undertaking job analyses was that compiled by Blum and Naylor (1968), which itemized ten different approaches to gathering information. However, each of these approaches suffers from some drawbacks, which suggests the use of combinations of techniques to overcome them. In the Komet scenario outlined above, different approaches to job analysis were used to identify the individual characteristics required. Initially this involved observing and questioning experienced workers and their managers to obtain an overview of all the tasks being carried out, as well as familiarization with the layout of the plant and the different types of machinery in use. This latter aspect can be very important at the interviewing and selection stages. The types of information the Komet team were interested in covered such topics as the various job titles, the number of people doing each type of job, and the person to whom the job holder was responsible. This information was further complemented by identifying the main purpose of each job, and recording each job holder's key responsibilities for other people, materials, money, tools and equipment, as well as the performance standards required, in terms of productivity, quality and return on capital.

Observations are one of the most frequently used approaches and, providing the observers are well trained, this approach can furnish high-quality information, although it is labour-intensive and costly, and suffers from some drawbacks. The first of these is that difficulties arise when observing jobs involving 'mental' work as there is little observable activity; in addition, some highly skilled manual jobs may involve actions that are too rapid to analyse, although this problem might be overcome with video techniques. Second, some employees may not wish all their actions to be observed, particularly if the job involves confidential information or some of the work is done at home in the evenings. Third, the analyst may record the observations incorrectly, using words and concepts not readily understood by the job holders, making verification very difficult.

One method called '*functional job analysis*' (FJA), developed by Fine and Wiley (1977), can overcome the latter problem, as it was expressly designed to control the language used to describe a job. FJA is predicated on the basis that work is always done in relation to data, people or things, and that each of these areas can be used to analyse a job on three levels (high, medium and low). In essence, the method utilizes a three-by-three matrix to guide analyses. Although FJA is pertinent to most methods of job analysis, it is particularly relevant to observational methods. A serious drawback is that it also requires four to five days' training in the use of the method, as it is fairly complex.

Two simpler job analysis methods are available based on the work of Levine (1983): combination job analysis method (CJAM), and brief job analysis method (BJAM). Both of these methods are based on the opinions of subject-matter experts (SMEs) who generate lists of tasks involved in a job, and then rate each task according to its difficulty level, how critical the task is and how long each task takes to complete. The importance of each task can then be assessed by multiplying the associated numerical values of these three components together. The SMEs can also generate a list of the knowledge, skills, abilities and other characteristics (KSAOs) necessary to the task, and rate them in a similar fashion to the task components, except that the ratings of the KSAOs would be determined by four features:

- how necessary these KSAOs are for new workers;
- how practical it is to expect employees to possess these features;
- how effectively particular KSAOs will distinguish between an average and an above-average worker;
- how many difficulties will arise from a worker lacking the necessary KSAOs.

These issues are particularly important. For example, if the Komet company had not identified the KSAOs necessary for new workers, they would not have been able to identify the five specific job groupings, and may well have selected personnel without the requisite abilities, leading to a higher staff turnover and longer training periods. Once again, however, a major drawback to pursuing this route is that the 'subject-matter experts' may not be true experts. This may result in unrealistic analyses of all the tasks.

Where the use of observations is impractical, such as in analyses of mental work, an alternative method may be the use of diaries or logbooks. This entails enlisting existing job holders to record all of their work activities for a specified time period on a daily basis. Because of the difficulties found in practice with this method, it is better to provide pre-printed logs or diaries with a system of headings. This offers the advantage of guiding and standardizing the entries, across job holders, although thorough preparation is essential as there is a danger of missing out crucial elements. Stewart (1967) provides an excellent example of the use of diaries. Some problems are associated with diary methods. First, short-cycle repetitive jobs, jobs involving speedy or intricate manual skills, and job holders unused to verbalizing their activities present particular difficulties. Ensuring that job holders faithfully complete their diary entry on a daily basis, instead of relying on their memory to make the entries a short time before the diaries are due to be handed in, presents another problem. Similarly, some job holders may report their jobs in minute detail, while others may simply give the gross details, as well as using different terminology for the same tasks. Thus it will be difficult to maintain consistent standards of reporting. Finally, analysing the data is likely to take a considerable amount of time because of the unstandardized nature of the entries.

Job-analysis questionnaires

Questionnaires are frequently used for job analysis. In the Komet example, two complementary questionnaires were used to provide information from two perspectives. Checklists, or 'job inventories' as they are sometimes called, are one of the simplest types of questionnaires. Typically, checklists contain large numbers of activities. Those which form a part of a job are ticked by job holders. Developing checklists requires thorough preparation, based on wide consultation and 'field trials' to ensure that the instructions, layout and scoring are easily understood, and that no crucial activities have been missed out. In practice the use of checklists is only feasible when there will be a large pool of respondents as subsequent analyses only focus on the proportion of job holders giving positive answers to the items. McCormick (1976) provides a set of guidelines for the development of checklists.

Many ready-made job-analysis questionnaires that are both reliable and valid are available for use. The Job Components Inventory (JCI), developed by Banks et al. (1983) in Britain, contains over 400 items concerned with the tools and equipment used, the perceptual and physical requirements, the levels of mathematical reasoning required, the communication and decision-making requirements, and the degree of responsibility involved in a job. It is most suited to jobs requiring limited skills and can easily be administered by trained personnel rather than job-analysis experts. The JCI takes about 45 minutes to complete.

Another British questionnaire is the Work Profiling System (WPS), developed by Saville and Holdsworth Ltd (1988), and updated in 1995 for use with personal computers. The basis of the questionnaire is a pool of over 800 items which reflect the attributes of jobs ranging from managerial and professional positions to manual and technical work. After choosing the appropriate level of job, a system is used to choose eight or more relevant sections for completion, so that in practice there are rarely more than 200 items to be answered. The WPS used in this way normally takes about an hour to complete. An example of a completed job analysis is provided in Figure 3.2.

The Positional Analysis Questionnaire (PAQ) was developed by McCormick et al. (1972) in the USA and is amongst the most widely used, probably due to its rigorous scientific development based on over 3700 jobs. One particular advantage is that each scale starts with a thorough description of the attribute being assessed, which is accompanied by a benchmark that can be used for comparison purposes. The PAQ is time-consuming to administer, some specialist knowledge is required, and computer analysis is also used.

Many other job-analysis questionnaires are available and the reader is referred to Spector et al. (1989) for a comprehensive review.

Major Sections / Task Category Titles	Mean	SD	N1	N2	Ranking Graph (9 8 7 6 5 4 3 2 1)
A: MANAGING TASKS					
A1: PLANNING	9.00	1.00	1	1	
A2: IMPLEMENTING / COORDINATING	6.00	4.00	1	1	
A3: CONTROLLING / DIRECTING	1.00	0.00	2	2	
A4: REVIEWING / EVALUATING					
B: MANAGING PEOPLE					
B1: SUPERVISING / DIRECTING	2.00	0.00	2	2	
B2: APPRAISING / EVALUATING					
B3: MOTIVATING	8.00	2.00	1	1	
B4: ASSISTING / CARING	6.50	3.50	1	1	
B5: HANDLING DISPUTES / GRIEVANCES	8.00	1.00	1	2	
B6: COUNSELLING					
B7: COOPERATING / LIASING					
C: GATHERING INFORMATION					
C1: INVESTIGATE / OBSERVE / SEARCHING	6.50	2.50	1	2	
C2: GATHERING INFORMATION					
D: THINKING CREATIVELY					
D1: ARTISTIC CREATIVITY					
D2: PROBLEM SOLVING / DESIGNING					
E: PROCESSING INFORMATION					
E1: ASSESSING / EVALUATING	4.00	0.00	2	2	
E2: ANALYSING / DIAGNOSING					
E3: INTEGRATING / CODING / ESTIMATING					
E4: CALCULATING	9.00	1.00	1	1	
E5: INTERPRETING	3.00	0.00	2	2	
E6: CHECKING					
E7: DECIDING					
E8: LEARNING / RESEARCHING					
F: COMMUNICATING					
F1: INFLUENCING / ADVISING					
F2: REPRESENTING / INSTRUCTING / BRIEFING	9.00	0.00	0	2	
F3: INFORMING / DISCUSSING / INTERVIEWING					
F4: WRITING / ADMINISTRATING					
F5: REPRESENTING / SELLING					
F6: PR / DEVELOPING RELATIONSHIPS	9.00	0.00	0	2	
G: PHYSICAL ACTIVITIES					
G1: PHYSICAL ACTIVITIES / VEHICLES					
G2: USING TOOLS / MACHINERY					

Figure 3.2   Work Profiling System example
Source: Courtesy of Saville and Holdsworth Ltd

EVALUATIVE PERFORMANCE CRITERIA

Whichever method or combination of job analysis methods is used, the primary functions are to develop a job description that is agreed by all those involved and to provide a basis for generating personnel specifications to aid in selection decisions. Once the analysis is complete there is a strong temptation to proceed directly to personnel specifications. However, an additional step that is required, but often ignored, is the development of evaluative performance criteria based on the job description. These performance criteria will be useful at a later stage when the selection process is being validated. Validation (see Chapter 4) of a selection system is a time-consuming activity, and there are times when it is not wise for an organization to rely on a statistical validation of its procedures (e.g. when numbers are so small that sampling error might influence the analysis unduly). It is, of course, always sensible to keep good records and to monitor the success of selection decisions. Even with small numbers, if employees who were thought outstanding at interview are no better, on the job, than candidates who were marginal, this might signal problems with the selection, induction or training procedures. Whether for general monitoring or for more rigorous statistical purposes it is always necessary to know how well recruits are performing in their job.

At some stage someone, possibly in the courts or industrial tribunals, will ask whether the selection system works and whether or not it is valid. To be able to answer these questions with any certainty, it is necessary to compare the predictions made about future performance against actual performance criteria. Although it is possible to define the performance criteria after the selection process is complete, it is usually better to define them as soon as possible after the job analysis has been completed. Although it is often easier to choose criteria with the benefit of hindsight, if the performance criteria are chosen after the selection process is complete, there is a danger of bias resulting from choosing only those performance criteria that indicate success in the selection process. If this occurs there is a very real danger that the judiciary will always favour the unsuccessful applicant who takes a complaint to court on the grounds that the selection procedure unfairly discriminates between applicants (Hogan and Quigley, 1986).

Not only is it important that the job-performance criteria are specified in advance of the selection process, but it is also important that the performance criteria should be chosen with great care. The validation of the selection method may be severely contaminated otherwise. Pursell et al. (1980) provide an example of this when tests given to electricians were correlated with supervisory ratings of their performance. A correlation of zero was found, indicating that no relationship existed between the supervisory ratings of job performance and selection test performance. After the supervisors were trained in observation and communication techniques, better correlations were found. The typical correlation for supervisory ratings with results-oriented criteria is placed at 0.27 (Heneman et al., 1987). In this example, if the original supervisory ratings had been relied upon to establish validity, it is likely that the selection procedures used would have been considerably undervalued, and possibly discarded.

The above example illustrates the particular importance of relevant job performance criteria if the selection method used is to be successfully validated. The relevance of a performance criterion can be determined by the extent to which its use as an index of success is related to 'true' success in any given activity. Relevance is usually the first requirement when operationalizing a criterion, followed closely by its stability over time (reliability) and its availability and acceptability (practicality). See Chapter 4 for more detailed discussion on these issues.

In considering the choice of performance criteria, it is usually better in the first instance to be guided by the job description derived from the job analysis, as it will almost certainly contain explanations of the behaviours and actions the job holder will be expected to perform. These behaviours and actions are termed 'immediate-level criteria' and are normally used as a check to ensure that newly selected candidates are doing things in the right way and are behaving in the appropriate manner.

At the next level, 'intermediate criteria' are used that focus on the performance results expected of new hires, after a predetermined period of time. These criteria can be based on the current performance standards associated with the job, identified and specified previously in the job description. These standards might include the meeting of production or quality targets, the return on capital investment, or tests to demonstrate technical knowledge and skill on the job. It should be recognised, however, that organizational constraints may affect a job holder's performance levels, and that these will need to be taken into account when developing criteria (see Chapter 5). If a thorough job analysis has been conducted some, if not all, of these constraints will have been identified and should, therefore, be available to aid in the selection of the criteria. For example, the use of outdated equipment or lack of resources or stock may affect levels of performance. Similarly, jobs may entail short production runs and frequent changes in methods, design or setting-up procedures which affect absolute levels of performance. Thus, the influence of these constraints will contaminate the criteria used to assess the validity of the selection system.

The latter examples bring us to the third level of criteria, termed 'ultimate criteria'. These are essentially concerned with organizational features, and are used to assess how much a person contributes to organizational goals. For example, a good safety adviser would be expected to have a major impact on the organization's safety management system, to the extent that accident rates are consistently being reduced, making the organization's ultimate goal of 'zero accidents' more realistic. Other indices of ultimate criteria in an industrial setting might include net profit, productivity levels, organizational growth, an increase in market share, or meeting the legal requirements of statutory bodies. These criteria may be located by referring to company policy documents (see Table 3.1).

In practice, however, several problems may exist with assessments of ultimate criteria. The first of these is related to the fact that data may take several years to accumulate, and will therefore not be available in time to influence the selection system. Second, most choices of ultimate criteria are badly defined, leading to difficulties in measurement, although this can be mitigated by more specific criteria, derived from careful consideration of measurement issues. Third, the wider prevailing conditions such as the state of the economy, changes in government policy or in the company's markets may influence and contaminate the criteria. In practice it is recommended that where possible, beginning with immediate-level criteria, all three types of criteria be used to assess the efficacy of the selection system (see Table 3.1).

Traditionally, performance criteria are classified into three main types, reflecting production, judgemental and personnel data. Production data may be a useful and attractive source of criteria, particularly when these data are routinely collected for other purposes. For example, shopfloor productivity can be measured by counting the number of widgets each worker produces. The extensive proliferation of computers in the workplace enables the performance of many clerical functions to be monitored. For example, the efficiency of dispatchers, telephone operators, customer services clerks, etc., are easy to monitor using the very same equipment that helps these job holders to perform their duties and responsibilities. For many professional or managerial jobs, however, production data may not be so readily available, as, typically, they are involved in coordinating others or providing a service. If they produce anything it is likely to be in such small quantities that it would take several years, or even decades, to gather sufficient information to be useful. One important caveat when using production data is that production data normally reflects the performance of workgroups rather than individuals, which may present difficulties when an individual's

Table 3.1 Types of evaluative performance criteria

Levels of criteria	Immediate	Intermediate	Ultimate
Production	Number of units produced Time taken to produce units Number of errors in completed units Monetary value of sales Commission earnings Meeting deadlines Quality/quantity ratio	Number of times targets are reached Return on investment Effectiveness/efficiency of services Rate of errors	Contribution to organizational goals Meeting of legislative requirements Organizational growth indicators
Judgemental and observational	Behaviours and actions for effective job performance	Social competency Tests of job knowledge Tests of job skills Service orientation	Customer satisfaction surveys Employee satisfaction surveys Performance appraisals
Personnel	Time-keeping Sickness absence Accident involvement Disciplinary Grievances	Organizational commitment Turnover Absenteeism Overtime worked Bonuses achieved	Training achievements Promotion rate Salary regrading Physical/psychological health

performance is used to aid in validating the selection system.

Judgemental data, on the other hand, can be used to assess both groups and individuals and is relatively easy to collect, although it is not without its own problems. Judgemental data refer to ratings about someone's job performance and have been used in approximately 45 per cent of validity studies, partly because they are fairly easy to develop and use and partly because of the inaccurate assumption that line managers know their subordinates' jobs and the degree to which the job holder is competent. Although these ratings usually come from line managers, they can also come from peers, subordinates, observers or even be self-ratings by the job holder. Most ratings, however, suffer from a number of errors, irrespective of the type of rater. Typically these errors are concerned with 'halo effects', whereby a person who is rated very highly on one characteristic is subsequently rated highly on other characteristics purely on the basis of impressions of the original characteristic; with 'leniency', which refers to the tendency of raters always to score people very highly; with the 'error of central tendency' which occurs because raters tend to give average scores rather than make extreme judgements; with contrast effects, which contribute to rater error when a person is rated in comparison with others and a 'true' rating is not given.

Despite the extensive use of judgemental ratings from the 1930s to the 1970s, difficulties with judgemental errors were noted fairly early on. Attempts to minimize these errors led to the development of behaviourally anchored rating scales (BARS) (Smith and Kendall, 1963; Schwab et al., 1975) and the behavioural observation scale (BOS) (Latham and Wexley, 1977). The rationale for the development of behavioural scales was predicated on the belief that most rating errors arise from ill-defined characteristics, allowing too much leeway for the rater's own interpretations. When rating scales are anchored by specific behaviours, the leeway for interpretation is significantly reduced, resulting in much higher inter-rater agreement (see Figure 3.3).

Developing a behaviourally anchored scale is normally achieved by proceeding through the following five steps:

- identify and define critical aspects of job performance (which are usually derived from job analyses);
- specific behaviours related to good, average and poor job performance are rated by job holders, line managers or job experts;

- to produce a behaviourally anchored scoring scale, the specific behaviours are assigned numerical values in descending order of importance (from excellent [10] to very poor [1]);
- the scale is re-evaluated by all involved, and the behavioural anchors which produce large amounts of disagreement between raters are discarded;

Figure 3.3 Behaviourally anchored rating scale for effective project team manager

- the average scores of the remaining anchors are calculated, to ensure that the full range from good to bad is sampled.

Personnel data refers to information held about job holders in the personnel department. This type of criterion has been used in approximately 20 per cent of validity studies. Unfortunately, much of it is subjected to the vagaries of normal day-to-day organizational life and so its use poses formidable analytical problems. Many personnel criteria are concerned with attendance at work. These include the number of times someone is late for work and whether or not they attend work. Unless monitored by some mechanical 'clocking-in' procedure lateness is difficult to measure. 'Clocking-in' procedures can also be circumvented with the aid of colleagues, which makes them susceptible to measurement error. The use of absenteeism as a measure suffers from problems of frequency in that it is a relatively rare occurrence. On average, it is thought that only four out of a hundred workers are responsible for all the absenteeism in an organization, and only a small portion of the four are absent twice or more. Turnover, when someone leaves their company, is flawed as a criterion measure, despite the fact that it has been used in about 13 per cent of validity studies. This is partly because of its relative infrequency, and partly because turnover can be contaminated by too many other factors, such as poor training, supervision or induction. Alternatively, the person may simply have been offered other employment. Perhaps, the only environment in which turnover might be used more confidently would be in the military, although it is difficult to leave voluntarily prior to completion of a specified period. Accidents are sometimes used as a criterion, but they are also flawed because accidents are relatively infrequent events. Moreover, many accidents are caused by a combination of underlying organizational failings, not personal factors. All the above personnel criteria suffer either infrequency or contamination from other factors, which suggests that they should not be used to validate selection procedures.

One very promising criterion related to individual performance may well be the use of work-sample tests. They are often used as predictors (see Chapter 7) but are also ideally suited for use as criteria. The advantages of work-sample tests reside in their careful development. Moreover, they are administered in carefully controlled conditions and can be given to job holders who would be expected to demonstrate proficiency and competence. Their drawbacks reside in the fact that they are demanding to deliver and expensive to develop. However, if work sample tests have already been developed as predictors, then using them as criteria maximizes the benefit/cost ratio (see Chapter 5). The distinction between productivity, judgemental and personnel data is useful and may be further supplemented by considering three further types of criterion data: performance, attachment and well-being. Performance data would include productivity or judgemental data concerning performance. Attachment refers to criteria that are concerned with the relationship between the employee and the organization. These might include absenteeism, turnover, organizational commitment and other indicators of the strength of attachment of the employee to the organization. Data concerning well-being focus on different issues from all the earlier categories and concern aspects such as employee satisfaction, mental health and general physical or psychological health. These are increasingly important criteria for employers and employees alike, though they have only recently begun to be incorporated into models of the personnel selection process.

SUMMARY

Because of the difficulties encountered when predicting people's future job behaviour, it is essential that the relevant job attributes are properly assessed so that they can be measured. Job analysis is a methodology that allows the requisite skills and abilities to be identified to derive accurate job and personnel specifications. A number of approaches are available and include observations, diaries or logbooks, checklists and questionnaires. Irrespective of the job analysis method(s) used, job specifications should be written in very specific terms, and cover five basic types of information:

* the job title;
* the immediate objectives of the task;
* the actions required to complete the task;
* the tools, equipment or work aids used;
* the required performance standards.

Once this information is available it becomes possible to derive a personnel specification that states the qualities required of successful applicants. Without either one of these formal documents it is difficult to develop a quality selection procedure, because they form the benchmark by which applicants are assessed. Additionally, this information serves to establish the performance criteria with which to assess the validity of the selection procedure(s) at a later date.

4 Evaluative standards for selection methods

Due to the establishment of the single market within the European Union, 'Greatplay Inc.', a Canadian toy-manufacturing company, decided to establish a new plant in the UK in order to maintain and increase their market share. During the construction of the plant, the parent company asked a UK-based recruitment specialist to identify the qualities that would be needed for the various managerial positions. Utilizing the Job Analysis Checklist (Lewis, 1985), analyses of all the management positions in two of the Canadian company's sister plants were undertaken to derive both job and personnel specifications. From these it was concluded that different management styles were needed for different departments and levels of the organization. For example, the production departments required managers who were able to maintain tight supervision and control, while the sales department required people orientated managers, operating under a 'hands-off' approach. Similarly, a new chief executive officer (CEO) with considerable leadership qualities was required, whereas a tough administrator was required for the number two position. A meeting was held with other human resource specialists to discuss the different selection methods available, and to decide which method would be best for each level and function. This was achieved by assessing the four requisite evaluative standards of practicality, interpretability, reliability and validity, in addition to benefit/cost ratios. For all the management positions, with the exception of the CEO, various psychological tests, biodata and 'in-tray exercises' were to be used. Thereafter, applicants with potential were to be interviewed. A decision was made to retain the services of an executive search firm to find the new CEO.

A comprehensive job-related biodata questionnaire (see Chapter 8) was devised to facilitate the initial screening process of applicants as it has been shown to be a reliable and valid predictor of future job performance and turnover. Thereafter, batteries of psychological tests (see Chapter 8) that would be able to identify suitable applicants for the various managerial levels were chosen. The Job Choice Exercise (Stahl, 1983) was chosen for its ability to discriminate between managers performing well and poorly, as well as because it was sexually and racially neutral. In addition, the test takes only 20 minutes to complete. Similarly, a personality questionnaire, the Management Potential Scale of the California Psychology Inventory (Gough, 1984) was chosen for its ability to distinguish between managers who are socially adept, productive and goal-oriented, and those who tend to be erratic, moody and self-defeating individuals. In-tray exercises (see Chapter 7), used to evaluate applicants' supervision, planning and decision-making skills, were also chosen.

The biodata questionnaire was used as the basis for sifting out unsuitable applicants. Fifty potential managers were invited to attend the selection process. Each applicant completed the test battery and in-tray exercises. After this stage, twenty applicants were excluded from the selection process. The remaining thirty attended a series of structured interviews (see Chapter 6) with five separate interviewers. Inter-interviewer reliability checks were conducted to establish the interviewers' consensus as to the choice of candidates. These reached 88 percent, indicating a large amount of agreement between the different interviewers. Subsequently twenty-five of the candidates were hired. Follow-up assessments, one year later, of the performance of the management team vindicated the use of the various selection methods. Productivity was found to be 25 percent higher than in the corresponding Canadian plants. Surveys also showed that the workforce were more motivated and satisfied in their work. Further assessments at two and five years showed that, year on year, productivity was improving by 15 percent and that the company was increasing its market share by 3 percent.

In the above example, the needs of Greatplay Inc. were met because the personnel specialists took time to evaluate the available selection methods on the basis of four evaluative standards. By doing so they ensured that they focused upon candidates solely in terms of their ability to perform the job and the necessary personal characteristics required for the job. Follow-up assessments of the selected candidates' job performance demonstrated that this reflective approach had added considerable value to the organization as both productivity and market share continued to increase year on year. To accomplish this goal the company chose the most appropriate selection method(s) for each job function that reliably discriminated between applicants while also accurately predicting future performance.

The best way of making choices between the various selection methods or tests is to set out in advance the requirements that a selection procedure should meet to deliver the best recruits for a particular job (see Chapter 5). In practice, no matter which actual methods are chosen, systematic selection requires that they should meet certain standards, particularly those concerning reliability, validity, interpretability and practicality. It should also be emphasized that, because these standards apply to any measurement system, the methods used to assess the candidates' subsequent job performance must also possess these qualities otherwise validation of the selection procedure becomes entirely meaningless.

RELIABILITY

If personnel specialists are to place any confidence in the results of selection procedures, it is obviously very important to have reliable measuring instruments. Consistency of measurement is the fundamental underlying concept of reliability and as such it is a very important standard with which to evaluate any selection method. If a selection test or method is unreliable the selector may just as well use a pin or draw a name from a hat to select candidates, as it amounts to the same thing. In principle, the reliability of any measurement system could be established by repeatedly measuring the same object under the same conditions. This is because a mean score based on 100 administrations is more stable than any one single score, by virtue of the fact that 'freak' circumstances (e.g. a hangover) which may influence any one administration are balanced out; also, random variations in the scores due to misleading or poor test questions will be evened out. In essence, the more the results agree, the more reliable the measurement system is.

For example, suppose that Greatplay Inc. had tested two methods of employment interviewing on 100 people prior to their operational use: one involving standardized interviews which presented the same questions in the same order to each applicant, the other involving the traditional unstructured interview which allowed interviewers to ask any questions that they deemed appropriate. Assume that selector agreement regarding choice of candidates was found to be 95 percent for the structured interviews and 37 percent for the unstructured interviews. Clearly, the indications would be that structured interviews were the more reliable as they consistently led to higher levels of agreement between selectors.

Types of reliability

As it is impractical and expensive in most circumstances to estimate the reliability of a selection method by 'umpteen' administrations a different strategy is often required. For example, prior to operational use Greatplay Inc. might have chosen to establish the reliability of their in-tray exercises by administering them on two separate occasions to the same groups of existing job holders. Had they done so they would have estimated the method's reliability by correlating the two sets of scores with each other. Because a reliable measure should produce two very similar scores for each person the resulting correlation is used as an index of stability. The higher the correlation is the better the match will be between each set of applicants' scores and, therefore, the more reliable the method will prove to be. The strategy described for estimating the reliability of the in-tray exercise is referred to as *test–retest reliability* and its main purpose is to establish the stability of a measure over time (see Cureton, 1971). Essentially, this involves obtaining a set of applicant scores for a particular method, waiting for a specified period of time and then asking the same applicants to sit the same test again. The main disadvantages of this approach reside in the fact that applicants may learn from the first trial and improve their performance on the retest, which may lead to a reduced reliability coefficient. This suggests that the time interval between administrations of the measure is of crucial importance. In general, the shorter the time period the more likely that learning effects will play a part. Equally, if the time interval is too long, other factors such as experience might have an effect, which again may reduce the reliability of the measure. It is difficult to suggest an optimum time interval, but most test–retest studies involve an interval of between one and three months.

When there are two different versions of the same test or selection procedure a reliability coefficient can be estimated by correlating the scores obtained on one version with the other. This type of reliability is termed '*parallel form reliability*' but it is thought to be impractical for most purposes because of the costly, time-consuming process that is necessary to develop two separate forms of the measure. Therefore, the parallel form method is normally used only when two versions of a test exist for other reasons. Both versions need to be balanced with each other in terms of coverage, difficulty, quality of content, etc. If this is not the case the reliability coefficient obtained will simply be a reflection of the less satisfactory version, thereby masking the true reliability of the better version. This may lead to both versions being discarded for selection purposes, even if the better version is extremely reliable. Problems can also arise from the administration of the two measures. Unless applicants respond to both versions in the same manner, for example by being highly alert and giving sufficient thought to both versions, reliability will tend to be underestimated. Similarly, if applicants are in different mood states while responding to each version, reliability estimates may be inflated.

A more frequently used method, based on the logic of parallel forms is that of *internal consistency*. Instead of developing two parallel forms of the same test, one test is divided into two parts (e.g. odd and even numbers). The scores from the two halves of the test are then correlated with each other. The main advantage of this form of reliability is its convenience, resulting in lower overall costs. However, it is important to recognize that this form of reliability may have some limitations. Put simply, splitting the number of items in half for any given scale has the effect of reducing the reliability estimates, because short scales are less reliable than longer ones. This underestimate can be corrected with the Spearman–Brown formula (see Smith and Robertson, 1993). In practice, however, the use of computer programs such as SPSS (Statistical Package for the Social Sciences) obviates the need for employing the formula, because the reliability estimates may be derived from procedures that make use of all the items in a test. The most common indices of internal consistency are Cronbach's (1951) Alpha, which is used when the test items are scored on some form of rating scale, and the Kuder–Richardson (1937) which is used when the measure is scored on a yes/no basis. In effect, the mean values of all possible split-half reliabilities are computed by both methods, although the end result is a slight overestimate of the measure's overall reliability (approximately 3 per cent). Of all the different methods of assessing a test's reliability the most common choice for test publishers is that of internal consistency, utilizing Cronbach's Alpha or Kuder–Richardson.

Another important form of reliability, illustrated by the Greatplay Inc. example, is that of *inter-rater reliability* which is used to determine the amount of agreement between different raters. This is used mainly for interviews or other selection methods that rely on the selectors' judgements. Typically, raters are trained in the use of an unambiguous scoring system. Two raters then score a small representative sample of results. Any differences are discussed until both are in agreement as to how to score particular aspects. Both raters then independently score a full sample of applicants. The scores for each rater are then correlated with the other. An inter-rater reliability coefficient of greater than 0.8 is desirable, as this indicates 80 percent agreement between raters. Anything less than this indicates that something is going wrong somewhere. Obviously, the lower the reliability coefficient the more that is going wrong. Most likely it will be the case that, despite initial agreement on how to score particular aspects of candidate attributes, the different selectors are basing their judgments on slightly different criteria. For example, one may be placing more emphasis on the possession of educational qualifications, while others may be placing greater emphasis on practical work experience. Alternatively, one selector may be more lenient in scoring applicants than others. Consequently, it is very important to identify the rating feature that is reducing the reliability coefficient, and address the issues raised. Costly errors may be made if unreliable measures are used.

VALIDITY

Equally important is the concept of validity, which refers to the accuracy of measurement. For any measurement system to be accurate, it must measure what it purports to measure. If a measurement system proves to be highly reliable but does not provide accurate results then it has low validity and, despite being reliable, it is of poor quality. The validity of a test is an extremely important evaluative standard. Before any particular test is used for selection purposes, the selector must be satisfied that it is valid for its intended purpose by providing accurate measurements of the attribute(s) under investigation. This is a crucial point because predictions about a candidate's future performance are based on the results of such tests. Take, for example, the use of polygraph tests to screen job applicants for their honesty. In 1986 physicians subjected 1000 people to the polygraph: 500 were instructed to tell the truth and 500 directed to lie. The polygraph indicated that 185 of the truthful people were liars, while indicating that 120 of the liars were truthful. These results show that the polygraph is not a perfectly *valid* measure of honesty. It may be perfectly reliable and produce the same results each time it is used on a particular person. It is not valid because it is *wrong* and does not measure honesty with perfect accuracy.

Strictly speaking, validation is more concerned with *the interpretation of scores, arising from a particular selection test or method*, rather than the tests or procedures themselves. This is a central point, because it is possible for a test to be valid for measuring one thing, but not another. For example, designers of selection tests for trainee computer programmers typically use mathematical ability to predict future performance. However, because modern programming requires high levels of verbal reasoning, rather than mathematical ability (Penney and Lazzarini, 1979), these tests are invalid for selecting computer programmers. They may be valid, however, for assessing applicants for jobs where numerical ability is important. Consequently, validation can be done only in relation to the purpose for which the test is used.

Types of validity

The most important definitions of validity are those related to content, construct and criterion-related validity, each of which is an evaluative standard in its own right. It must be recognized, however, that a test or selection method should possess all three types of validity. Content validity is often divided into two separate facets: face validity and content validity proper. *Face validity* is concerned with people's perceptions of how well a test measures what it is supposed to measure and as such is not, in the true sense, a type of validity at all. Some may argue that face validity is unimportant (see Mosier, 1947, for a full discussion), but in reality it may be of the most practical importance, because it may cause a test to be rejected, either by the organization or by applicants. It has been proposed that despite the poor validities associated with ad hoc interviews, they are most commonly used because of their perceived face validity. *Content validity* as such is mainly a sampling issue related to the measure's development. The content in any given measure can be visualized as a sample of items, tasks or behaviours that reflect the construct being measured. Assuring content validity is a two-phased process. Phase one focuses on whether or not a selection method reflects all the known features of the job in question (e.g. interpersonal skill, extroversion, etc.). This is normally achieved by comparing the measuring instrument against the job and person specifications derived from job analyses. Phase two assesses how well all the tasks featured in the measuring instrument accurately reflect the attributes of what is being measured. For example, if a test was meant to measure general arithmetical ability but did not include any items on addition or subtraction, its content validity would be low. If, however, the same test was designed only to measure an applicant's multiplication and division ability, its content validity could well be high.

Construct validity is potentially the most useful but typically the most evasive and complex of the various types of validity. Cronbach and Meehl (1955) define a construct as 'some postulated attribute of people presumed to be reflected in test performance'. As such this type of validity attempts to answer the question, 'What is the psychological meaning of the scores, and how do the scores relate to other measures?' Construct validity is, therefore, more concerned with the degree of correspondence between the proposed construct and reality. Take, for example, the Job Choice Exercise developed by Michael Stahl in 1983 and used by Greatplay Inc. to provide an indication of managerial motivation. Managerial motivation is not a physical entity but merely a label used to describe the strength and direction of someone's behaviour, consisting of two further constructs: the Need for Power (NPow), a descriptive label reflecting a need to influence others, and Need for Achievement (NAch), a descriptive label reflecting the need to set and achieve goals. In order to validate these constructs, Stahl tested the hypothesis that someone with high managerial motivation would score high on both the NPow and NAch scales, and vice versa. He tested the measure on 1417 respondents from a variety of occupations, both blue-collar and managerial positions, across a range of differing industries. He found that those who scored high on these two constructs had a higher promotion rate than low scorers, that high scorers were more likely than low scorers to be leaders, and that high scorers were more likely than low scorers to be managers. From these results we can infer that the construct of managerial motivation has considerable credence. In essence, therefore, Stahl tested the construct validity of *the idea behind the test*, rather than the test itself. As in this case, however, it is often difficult to separate the validation evidence provided by this approach from evidence of the criterion-related validity of the measure itself. A more clear-cut method for establishing the construct validity of a newly developed test is to correlate the new test scores with the scores of another established test that is believed to accurately reflect the construct involved. For example, the construct validity of an extroversion test could be established by correlating the new measure of extroversion with an established test of extroversion. The construct validity of a measure can also be determined with statistical techniques such as exploratory and confirmatory factor analysis, with the aid of computer programs. However, these techniques are beyond the scope of this book and the reader is referred to Joreskog and Sorbom (1988), Bentler (1989), or Ferguson and Cox (1993).

Knowledge of the construct validity of a test can also aid in judgements of a test's likely *criterion-related validity*. As demonstrated in the Greatplay Inc. example, criterion-related validity is concerned with the links between the test used and job performance on some criterion (e.g. meeting production targets). How closely the test is related to *subsequent* performance is defined as the test's *predictive validity*. Establishing the predictive validity of a new test can, however, involve a certain amount of risk as well as being costly. For example, suppose Greatplay Inc. had developed a new test of managerial motivation and hired applicants on the basis of the test scores, and after a period of time they had decided to assess each applicant's performance in the job and correlate the scores with the original test scores. Suppose they obtained low correlations. Because the match between the original test and performance scores indicates the predictive validity of the test, Greatplay Inc. would find that they had hired many unsuitable applicants. Therein lies the risk that many companies are reluctant to take because of the costs involved. A practical way to overcome this problem is to administer the new test to all applicants, but select them on the basis of other, established, methods. After a period of time, the performance scores of the successful applicants should be correlated with their scores on the new test. If a high correlation is found, indicating that the test has predictive validity, the test can be used in subsequent selection procedures. Needless to say, the resulting validity coefficient will be affected by the accuracy of both the new test itself and the measures used to assess performance. This is an important point as it is often the case that most effort is directed at establishing the accuracy of the new test, while the measures by which performance (see Chapter 3) will be assessed are largely ignored.

Another procedure for assessing criterion-related validity is that of establishing *concurrent validity*. This involves administering the selection measure to existing employees and measuring their current performance in the job. These two scores are then correlated with each other. The advantages of this method are related to both the speed with which the validity of the measure can be established and the lower costs. However, this method also suffers from some disadvantages: first, because existing employees are not likely to be as motivated as applicants seeking a job they may not respond correctly, which may lead to inaccurate estimates of the validity coefficient; and, second, existing employees are more likely than not to be good at their jobs, because those who were not will have been moved to other work, or may have left the company. This means that the range of scores obtained on the test might be restricted, which nearly always results in a lower validity coefficient than is truly the case. This latter problem can be corrected with mathematical formulae (see Smith and Robertson, 1993). A special type of concurrent validity that may overcome these disadvantages is referred to as the *nominated groups technique*, and is based on the use of two groups of people who are known to differ in the characteristics the test is supposed to measure. For example, it may be that older workers are known to have a better attendance record and have fewer absences than younger people because they are more conscientious. A test of conscientiousness would be devised and administered to groups of both younger and older people. If the measure were valid, a clear difference in scores between the groups should emerge, with older people scoring much higher. If no differences were found between the two groups, the measure would be invalid.

INTERPRETABILITY

Developing a reliable and valid selection method does not guarantee that good applicants can be distinguished from poor applicants. For this to occur applicants must also be graded in some way. Because grading is normally based on test scores it is particularly important that an applicant's scores reflect their ability. For example, if a selection interview or ability test were such that every applicant passed, or so difficult that every applicant failed, the selector would not be able to 'see the wood for the trees'. An important quality standard, therefore, is the degree to which the scores on a test accurately reflect applicants' abilities and enable distinctions to be made between them. The more they do so the better the quality and the more interpretable and useful the test will be.

Interpretation of an applicant's test scores is normally achieved in either of two main ways: *criterion-based or norm-based scoring systems*. In criterion-based systems an applicant's scores are compared against some standard to indicate an absolute level of performance such as 'pass' or 'fail'. A typist's speed (40 words per minute) and accuracy (no errors) are such an example. With norm-based scoring systems an applicant's test scores are judged in relation to other applicants, existing job incumbents or some more general sample of people. The choice of scoring system is mostly determined by the requirements of the job and person specifications derived from job analyses.

Criterion-based scoring systems

Typically, criterion-based scoring systems are used when a selection test has been designed to reveal what an applicant can do. Features common to most criterion-based measures are that:

- test items tend to be highly specific in terms of the behaviour or levels of performance required;
- the tests tend to tap into the knowledge base underpinning the required behaviours;
- success is usually determined on a pass-or-fail basis, although in some instances this may be organized into various levels or grades of performance;
- candidates are allowed several attempts until they succeed, although further tuition is often required between attempts (e.g. the driving test).

Work-sample tests (see Chapter 7) are a prime example of a criterion-based approach to assessing performance. The various components of skill (criteria) required of an advanced scaffolder, for example, include the ability to work at great heights while carrying loads heavier than the scaffolder's own weight; to place 21-foot tubes vertically on top of one another; to design and erect different types of scaffold such as 'cantilevers' and 'flying shores'; to work to design engineer's 'blueprints', etc. Knowledge of safety aspects and 'loading' stresses is also required. Construction Industry Training Board (CITB) tests require assessments of a scaffolder's competence in all these skills. A failure in any one of them means a failure of the whole test. The scaffolder's performance is not judged in relation to others, but purely on his or her own performance. In principle, therefore, any applicant may pass or fail.

Norm-based scoring systems

Because personnel selection is often competitive in nature, selectors almost always wish to know how applicants match up against each other. Interpreting one applicant's performance scores in relation to other applicants is best achieved with norm-based scoring systems. For example, based on a sample of 1417 respondents, the Job Choice Exercise (Stahl, 1983) indicates that the norms for highly motivated managers are scores above 3.14 on both the Need for Power (NPow) and 4.64 on the Need for Achievement (NAch) scales. Applicants who score less than these values on both scales have been found to be low in managerial motivation.

The first type of norm-based scoring system relevant to personnel selection is that of *positional scoring systems* which refer to the grading of an applicant in relation to others. The grading of applicants is usually based on a *table of norms* which shows how other people have previously scored on the same measure. For example, an organization recruiting management trainees would compare the scores of this year's intake with the scores obtained by previous intakes. However, developing norm tables requires great care (see Bethell-Fox, 1989) and a reasonably large sample, usually not less than 400 people.

A number of different types of positional scoring systems exist, some more useful than others. The most basic are those where an applicant's score is simply graded as above or below average, or ranked in descending order from best to worst. The advantage of these methods is that they are both simple and quick. The disadvantage is that they are also very crude and result in a huge waste of information. Consequently they should be used only as a last resort. Ranks, for example, do not indicate levels of competence or merit. A top-rank placing may just mean that the applicant is the best of a bad bunch. Alternatively, a place on the bottom rank could mean that the applicant is only slightly worse than a group of excellent applicants. Moreover, the ranks may actually distort and exaggerate any differences between applicants, by minimising large differences and magnifying small ones, making it very difficult to analyse the ranking system in a meaningful way.

A more sophisticated positional scoring system is based on the use of percentile ranks which attempt to place an applicant in a representative queue, relative to 99 others. For example, a position on the 80th percentile indicates that an applicant's test scores are equal to or higher than 80 percent of the other applicants. The advantages of percentile scores are twofold:

- an applicant can be compared with all the other applicants on a particular test;
- an applicant's scores on different tests can be readily evaluated in relation to each other.

For example, a percentile score of 75 on an aptitude test is better than a percentile score of 65 on an ability test. The main disadvantage of percentile scores is that they are only a method of ranking the relative achievement of applicants within a particular test, not a measure of differences between applicants' test scores.

Unlike positional scoring systems, *standardized scoring systems* take into account both the grading of applicants and the differences between them. As such they provide a more accurate and meaningful assessment of relative achievement by using *standard scores* which not only indicate where an applicant's scores lie in relation to the mean score of all the applicants on a particular test (i.e. above or below the mean score) but also show how far their scores differ from the mean score. The advantages of using standard scores to discriminate between applicants are threefold, in that they:

- identify where an applicant is placed in relation to others;
- identify the magnitude of difference between test scores;
- avoid the distortion or exaggeration of differences between applicants.

Thus the analysis and interpretation of test scores are made somewhat easier. (Readers who wish greater understanding of norm-based scoring systems are referred to Appendix A.)

PRACTICALITY

For any selection method to be of practical use it makes sense that it measures what it is supposed to measure, and predicts what it is supposed to predict. In addition to its accuracy and predictive powers, however, the practicality of a method is assessed from two further perspectives: its perceived usefulness and fairness, and the extent to which it devours organizational resources. Both of these features are evaluative standards, and as such are likely to have a bearing upon subsequent decisions. If the chosen method has limited usefulness and/or appears to unfairly discriminate against applicants (e.g. on the grounds of gender, ethnicity or educational levels), or the costs outweigh any potential benefits, operational use of the method ought to be discontinued.

Decisions about the acceptability of a particular selection method ought to be made at the design stage of a selection procedure (see Chapter 5). Initially, evaluations will normally be made by selection specialists within the human resource department, as their expertise and technical knowledge provide a sound basis for determining a method's value. However, other parties potentially involved in the selection process should also be included. Senior management should certainly be involved, partly because they decide the allocation of resources, and partly to gain their interest and commitment. Piloting the method with current applicants before its operational use for selection purposes is also important. If applicants are uncomfortable with it they may respond in ways that distort the results, and thereby diminish its usefulness. For example, very different results will be found for in-tray exercises conducted alone in a quiet room compared to being watched by the other applicants in a noisy room. Similarly, the perceptions of political and other pressure groups may play a part if the method is thought to discriminate unfairly against ethnic or other minority groups. For example, Kellet et al. (1994) reported that British Rail (BR) changed its assessment practices after being taken to court. Eight train guards at London's Paddington station, with the support of the Commission for Racial Equality, took BR to court because of the adverse impact the assessments had on ethnic minorities. Similar problems had also been identified at London Underground. As a result of the litigation, both companies changed their practices after reaching 'out of court' settlements. This example aptly demonstrates the importance of evaluating the practicality of selection instruments in terms of their usefulness and consumption of resources prior to their operational use.

THE CONSTRUCTION OF TESTS

Many different types of selection tests are available, the most common being cognitive tests, personality questionnaires and work-sample tests. Although these can often be purchased from specialist test developers, it may be necessary to develop a test 'in-house'. The development of any type of test is more to do with systematic preparation and the following of a logical sequence than anything else. The basics of test development are described below, but they are not intended to be exhaustive because it can involve quite complex and sophisticated procedures. However, they do serve to provide some insight into the process, so that those considering purchasing commercial tests or developing in-house tests can appreciate what is involved and are more fully informed. The interested reader is referred to Cronbach and Glesser (1965) for a fuller description.

The questions in any test must be written and chosen with great care, but a good rule of thumb is to keep them as simple and clear as possible. While the vocabulary used should also be carefully aimed at the target audience, it is also important to keep out unnecessary items or items with two or more questions embedded in them as they are confusing to the respondent and make interpretation difficult. A good procedure for satisfying the above requirements is to go through the question bank, item by item, and ask what purpose each item serves. For example, if a test is being designed to measure the analytical ability of trainee accountants, it would be wise to consider what 'analytical ability' means. It way well be that much of the trainee's job will be extracting information from tables, graphs or pie charts. Therefore, to ensure content validity the test might be constructed so that it measures an applicant's ability to extract meaning from such tables and graphs, when certain information is approximate or even missing. Care must be taken, however, to ensure that each test item reflects only those constructs being measured. Attempts should also be made to visualize how each question might be scored as this will have some bearing on the type of scoring format chosen.

A number of scoring formats are available, and the choice of these is as important as the choice of question items themselves, as they are the bedrock by which applicants will be accepted or rejected. They range from simple yes/no responses to ratings on some type of bipolar scale, each with their own advantages or disadvantages. Yes/no responses are easier than multiple-choice answers but they suffer from less discriminatory power, although increasing the length of a test may compensate for this. Multiple-choice items are good at discriminating between applicants and are often used in cognitive tests, such as knowledge or aptitude tests. Multiple-choice items also allow precise scoring, since the answer can only be right or wrong. Their main disadvantage resides in the difficulty of generating distracter items (i.e. wrong answers) that are plausible but difficult. If the correct answer is too obvious, the discriminatory power of the test will be severely diminished. Bipolar scales are commonly used and comprise statements or characteristics that the applicant rates in terms of their agreement or disagreement.

Once the questions and scoring formats have been chosen, they need to be compiled into a user-friendly format, with clearly written instructions and an example question, so that test users fully understand what is required of them to complete the test. Very often, at this stage of development, there will probably be more questions than are necessary. Estimates suggest that there will be about three times as many as will form the final test or measure. The initial measure is then piloted on a relatively large sample of existing job holders to ensure that the questions are easily understood.

Ascertaining the discriminatory value of the items is achieved by correlating each individual item score with the total test, or subscale, score. Items with high correlations are usually retained, and those with low correlations are discarded (see Guilford and Fruchter, 1978 for a fuller discussion on item analysis). Once the suitability of the items has been determined, a final version is compiled. Knowledge tests usually begin with easy questions and get progressively more difficult throughout the test. With tests designed to measure attitudes and personality, it may be useful to mix up negatively and positively worded items, in order to avoid people responding in an unthinking manner.

The final stage involves administering the test to a large representative sample to establish its norms, reliability and validity, prior to its use as a selection instrument. In addition, the test's fairness should also be established to ensure it does not unfairly discriminate against subgroups of the population, e.g. on the basis of gender or ethnic group.

INTEGRATION

In practical terms, the more reliable and valid a measure or selection method is the greater its value in accurately predicting someone's performance in the job for which he or she is being selected. How then does one ensure and evaluate the reliability and validity of a selection method? If we take the case of structured interviews, the initial steps involve the use of job analyses to develop a set of dimensions, competencies and constructs (e.g. interpersonal relations, business skills, etc.) so that replies at interview can be rated on these. Subsequently, a series of standard job-related questions are derived that ask candidates how they would behave in various realistic job situations. The answers to these should be graded (refer to Chapter 6 for more details) or classified in some systematic way (e.g. with a rating scale) so that the interviewer knows what a good or poor response is. This leads to a consistent, objective scoring of responses which helps to maximize the reliability and validity of the selectors' judgements, as well as helping to standardize the overall process. This feature of standardization is important, as it allows a direct comparison of responses between applicants. Thereafter, it would be a good idea to ensure that the proposed interviewers attended some form of standardized interview training, involving opportunities for practice, discussion and feedback. This is important, as the levels of agreement between interviewers are likely to be much greater after training. Taking the issue of standardization further, during the interviews each candidate should be asked the same questions. Not only does this aid selection decisions but it also helps to ensure fairness across applicants. If two or more interviewers are involved in assessing individual candidates, it is possible, and highly desirable, to check the inter-interviewer reliability by ascertaining the degree to which the interviewers agree on candidate suitability. By following a standardized procedure as outlined above the reliability of the interview will be considerably enhanced.

Evaluating the criterion-related validity of the interview is another matter. This will often need to be done at some later date, but in essence it involves assessing the selected candidates' performance in the job against relevant performance criteria (see Chapter 3). In some settings following a concurrent approach and validating the interview by using current employees would be a less time-consuming practical alternative. The higher the degree of overlap between good job performance and performance at the interview, the higher is the validity of the method. In general, a validity coefficient above 0.5 is excellent, 0.4–0.49 is good, and 0.3–0.39 is acceptable. Validity coefficients below 0.3 are not always adequate, although in some circumstances validities of less than 0.3 are of value.

In principle, assessing the reliability and validity of other selection methods follows more or less the same procedures as for the interview. The first stage involves the determination of factors necessary for successful job performance, based on a thorough job analysis of the job in question. These factors are then used to derive measures (psychological paper-and-pencil, work-sample or in-tray exercises) of an applicant's ability to do the job, and the performance criteria by which validity assessments are made at a later date. Subsequently the applicants are assessed. The performance of those chosen is assessed at a later date. The scores obtained at the selection stage are then correlated with work-performance assessments. For concurrent validity, a group of existing job holders are assessed on both selection and performance measures at the same time. The higher the degree of overlap between the selection scores and the performance assessments, the higher the validity, and therefore the more useful the method in accurately selecting the best candidates (all other things being equal). Throughout this chapter it has been assumed that the criterion against which a selection method is validated (to establish criterion-related validity) is work performance. Sometimes the relevant criterion is not performance but some other aspect of work-related behaviour, such as absenteeism or tenure. It is also useful, in many settings, to validate selection methods against criteria that are more specific than *overall* work performance, such as managerial skills, problem-solving ability or business acumen. Whatever criteria are relevant, the procedures described earlier in the chapter remain appropriate. When looking at the results of research or in-company validation studies, it is important to check what criteria have been used to validate the method. It is less than optimum to use a measure that has been validated against tenure to assess candidates' potential work proficiency.

SUMMARY

If the personnel function is to optimize its decision-making procedures to ensure that things are right first time, the four evaluative standards outlined in this chapter must be met by any selection method used. Time should be taken to develop fully the methods and tests to ensure that they are reliable, accurate and able to be properly interpreted, while also avoiding unfair discrimination against ethnic minorities and other social groups. Although the reliability of a selection device may be evaluated in different ways, the basic aim of each approach is to establish how well it produces consistent measurements of the features under investigation. Validity, on the other hand, is concerned with how accurate the selection device is, and is assessed from three complementary perspectives. However, even if a selection device has reached the necessary standards for reliability and validity, it must also meet the standards for interpretation of applicant scores as they form the basis for decision-making. The benefit/cost ratio of a selection procedure is also an extremely important standard and is the focus of the next chapter.

5 Establishing standards for selection procedures

Human resource specialists in a large banking corporation, 'MoneyBox' were confronted with a problem. Because they employed large numbers of graduates every year, they had decided to improve the effectiveness of their decision-making by adopting structured situational interviews derived from job analyses to replace the current approach of application forms, ad hoc interviews and references checks. The HR staff had spent a lot of time and money to develop the job analyses, leading to structured interview questions. Unfortunately, they had proceeded to the point of actually training 'in-house' trainers without seeking senior-management approval. A presentation meeting had been set for the following week, but the HR staff were worried that the necessary approval would be denied. A board director had already cast doubts on the value of the job analyses and the time and resources devoted to them, and was not sure that training line managers was necessary or worthwhile.

One member of the HR department knew of the existence of formulae that enabled the financial benefits from selection procedures to be estimated. She suggested that perhaps the best way of gaining approval was to demonstrate the value of good selection by calculating the return on investment. This involved a forecast of the number of recruits needed, the number of applicants that would be interviewed for each vacancy in order to determine the selection ratio, the average time that staff stayed with the organization, the annual worth to the company of each recruit in productivity terms, and the criterion-related validity of the selection instrument. Finally the costs involved had to be estimated so that they could be deducted.

The results of the application of the cost–benefit formulae to the estimated figures were illuminating. Over the next four years, current spending on recruitment and selection would cost the MoneyBox corporation £4.5m, with a forecast financial gain to the company of £52m compared to random selection. If they obtained management's approval to introduce structured situational interviewing, it would cost £4.8m to recruit the same number of graduates, but the forecast financial gains rose to £67m. A direct comparison of the costs between the current selection procedures and those proposed revealed that after tax adjustments the difference in costs was £336,000, with a net benefit difference of £15m. This represented a return on investment of 45 times the additional costs, or an extra £15,000 per recruit, per year. Using capital budgeting techniques to discount the effects of inflation and tax, the anticipated performance improvements resulting from situational interviewing over the next four years produced a £13.35m net present value. The HR director presented these figures at the meeting. The CEO and others were astonished to see the speed with which their investment in training line management in situational interviewing would pay off.

ESTIMATING RETURN ON INVESTMENT

Based on a real case study (Janz, 1989b), the MoneyBox banking scenario illustrates recent advances in personnel selection utility theory, which have made it possible to identify clearly the financial benefits that flow from different HR activities. In the past, many HR practices were difficult to quantify, and the benefits that flowed from them were often seen as intangible and difficult to pin down. This placed HR specialists at a disadvantage, compared to other management functions, in determining the potential financial benefits of their policies and practices.

In essence, selection utility models are decision-making aids that provide a consistent and structured framework within which to compare the outcomes of various decision options (Boudreau, 1989). Typically, selection utility models are seen as cost–benefit analyses, and as such the outcomes are usually explained to others in financial terms. The main focus of utility analysis is not on whether a particular individual should be hired, but on whether or not a particular set of selection procedures (e.g. unstructured interviews as opposed to work-sample tests) will enhance the productivity of the organization and produce a reasonable return on investment (ROI). Utility models aid decision-makers in determining the financial impact of their selection procedures on the organization as a whole. Typically, this amounts to the value added to the organization from recruiting high-performing applicants with good selection methods, compared to the value added to the organization from less accurate selection methods. Accordingly, the benefit/cost ratio is an important efficiency standard.

The basic utility model

Selection utility models can be expressed in terms of three basic attributes:

- *Quantity* refers to the number of staff to be recruited with a particular selection procedure over a period of time.
- *Quality* reflects the outcomes associated with particular selection procedures.
- *Costs* reflect the resources consumed by the selection procedures.

Estimates of financial gain (ROI) are derived from the product of quantity and quality minus cost. Generally speaking, the selection procedure producing the most gain is preferable. (Interested readers are referred to Appendix B for a worked example and the formulae to calculate benefit/cost ratios.)

In order to place the benefits expected from good selection procedures in context, it is often useful to provide a point of comparison. This point is usually derived from estimates of financial gain expected if the employing organization randomly selected people without regard to their skills or abilities. In most organizations, however, selection is not random and some attempts are made to select the better candidates for the job. Thus it is not uncommon to find comparisons being made between existing selection procedures and potential alternatives, as was the case in the MoneyBox example where structured interviews were developed on the basis of job analyses to replace traditional ad hoc interviews.

Quantity

Calculating selection benefit/cost ratios usually begins with determining how many vacancies there are to be filled. Although this may range from less than 5 per year in small companies to more than 100 in larger organizations, the precise number of vacancies will either be known or can be estimated from manpower planning models. However, because selection systems are rarely used for only one individual or in only one year, it is likely that a company's selection procedure(s) will be used more than once. In principle, therefore, the greater the number of vacancies filled with a particular selection procedure, the better the benefit/cost ratio will be.

Similarly, the longer the time period that new hires stay with an organization, the more the potential financial benefits of good selection will accrue year on year. Thus, when calculating the total worth of the selection method to the organization, it is necessary to estimate the average tenure of employees from personnel records.

Before the actual financial gains from personnel selection can be estimated, the cash value of one standard deviation (SD_y) in performance also has to be calculated. On the basis of empirically determined relationships between mean salary and mean work output, Hunter and Schmidt (1982) proposed that, as a rule of thumb, the monetary value of one standard deviation in job performance (SD_y) was equivalent to between 40 and 70 per cent of the salary related to the job vacancy. Because conservative estimates tend to be more credible with decision-makers, most applications of this rule of thumb err on the side of caution by using 40 per cent of salary as the benchmark when calculating SD_y. In many instances, however, 40 per cent of salary may be patently false. For example, the SD_y for operative jobs is closer to 20 per cent, while the SD_y for higher-level executive jobs may be nearer to 60 per cent. Nonetheless, if we accept this rule of thumb, it becomes relatively easy to convert the standard deviation of performance into monetary terms. For example, a starting salary of £14,000 per annum would give us an SD_y estimate of £5,600 p.a. Obviously, the larger the value of SD_y, the greater the potential gain, making it more worthwhile to expend effort to optimize selection procedures on jobs that have more impact on the organization.

Quality

When the number of applicants for each vacancy is large, the organization has the opportunity to select the highest quality applicants. The number of applicants invited to attend a selection procedure in proportion to the number of vacancies that need to be filled is referred to as the 'selection ratio'. Although larger numbers of applicants will tend to increase recruitment costs, good selection depends upon having more applicants than there are jobs. If it is necessary to recruit every applicant (i.e. the selection ratio is one), then no gains are possible. Therefore, the greater the number of applicants invited to attend for each vacancy, the smaller the selection ratio will be and the greater the potential gain to an organization from selecting a small group of good candidates from a larger group of applicants. In essence, therefore, the selection ratio reflects the calibre or quality of those selected, and can be used to determine the cut-off point between accepts and rejects.

Similarly, the selection ratio can be used to estimate the average performance of the successful applicants. In essence, because work performance is normally distributed, ranging from very poor to very good, with average performers falling in the middle of the range, above-average candidates would be expected to exhibit above-average work performance. Of course, in practice, some candidates thought to be above average will not produce above-average work performance – unless selection was perfect.

Because perfect selection is rare (as it depends on a perfect relationship between the selection method and the criterion-related measure of work performance) it is often necessary to scale down estimates of the average performance output of the successful applicants. Because the benefits to be obtained from personnel selection increase in proportion to the validity of the selection method used, this is achieved by using validity coefficients (see Chapter 4) to scale down the expected benefit. Accordingly, the better the criterion-related validity of the selection method, the greater the potential financial gain.

Costs

The costs of the selection procedure also need to be calculated so that they can be subtracted from the estimated gains. Costs can be direct or indirect. Direct costs include those associated with recruitment, the screening of applicants, the selection method and procedures, travel and accommodation, etc. Indirect costs include long-term interest rates, corporation tax and wage inflation (see Boudreau, 1989). The adjustments for these factors are normally done with capital budgeting techniques, the expertise for which normally resides in an organization's finance department. It is worth mentioning at this juncture that, if these indirect costs are taken into account when others such as production, marketing, etc., do not consider them, then the financial gains may appear low in comparison to the other estimates.

Once all of the quantity, quality and cost parameters have been estimated, it becomes relatively simple to calculate the potential financial gains (ROI), by multiplying each individual parameter by the other parameters (see Appendix B for a worked example).

Applications

As the MoneyBox example illustrated, utility analysis not only offers the human resource specialist the opportunity to compete for organizational resources on a level footing with other managerial functions, which hitherto has been somewhat difficult, but also allows for more informed decision-making. For example, utility calculations could be made concerning the effects of a declining or expanding labour market on an organization's recruitment strategies, or to determine advertising strategies for vacant posts. As the previous material has shown, the bigger the field of candidates the better the financial gain. It is quite simple to use utility analysis to explore the benefits associated with attracting more candidates (which would improve the selection ratio) and compare this against the costs involved in the advertising campaign. Similarly, utility analysis could be applied to other human resource interventions, such as training, performance appraisals, participation and incentive schemes.

OPTIMIZING THE DESIGN OF SELECTION PROCEDURES

As illustrated by the MoneyBox example, significant financial gains depend to a large extent on optimal selection procedures. In practice, however, selection procedures are usually determined by the preferences of the human resource specialist, rather than by a systematic evaluation of the procedures available. This may partially explain why the least reliable and valid selection methods (i.e. traditional interviews and references) are so widely used (Robertson and Makin, 1986; Shackleton and Newell, 1991). Systematic evaluation, however, involves the application of certain principles for defining, shaping and maintaining the optimal selection procedure. Based on the principles of an engineering design cycle model, Roe (1984, 1989) provides a selection technology by which the systematic evaluation of the component parts of an existing or proposed selection procedure is made possible. The main strength of this type of selection technology is its flexibility, as it can be simultaneously applied, for example, to the design of selection methods, job-analysis instruments, or the whole selection procedure.

Functions of selection procedures

Before an organization's selection procedures can be fully optimized, however, it is useful to know the functions that each component serves, as they tend to shape the final procedure. Roe and Grueter (1989) identified four main functions:

* information-gathering;
* prediction;
* decision-making;
* information supply.

The information-gathering function is used mainly to obtain information about job opportunities, job content, job requirements, etc., and the personal characteristics required of applicants (see Chapter 3). It is also useful to focus on contextual information such as the nature and location of the organization, career structures, types of employment contracts, working hours and conditions of employment, time and resource constraints. The prevailing political and organizational culture may also be important. The types of information that might be needed will depend to a large extent on the nature

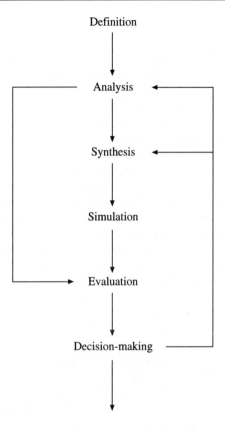

Figure 5.1   The design cycle model for selection procedures
Source: Based on Roe (1984, 1989)

of the job, the labour market situation, and the relative bargaining position of both organization and candidate. As a rule of thumb, however, it is worth being guided by cost–benefit considerations in order that the effort involved in gathering the information can be balanced against its usefulness within the organization.

The predictive function is more concerned with transforming information about an applicant's present qualities into predictions about their future work behaviour for the benefit of the organization (see Chapter 4). Typically this involves choosing the most appropriate selection method(s) for the job(s) in question (See chapters 6, 7, 8 and 9).

The decision-making function is concerned with transforming predictive information about applicants into action (i.e. accept/reject) (see Chapter 10). This may entail making choices between statistical and judgemental decision-making. For example, adopting a maximum-risk strategy might be appropriate in entrepreneurial organizations where a highly talented individual is sought, and the firm is willing to risk failures. Conversely, large, well-established corporations may wish to play safe and minimize risk by selecting average applicants.

The information-supply function serves as a feedback mechanism to all those involved in the procedure, to enable further modifications or improvements. This will include informing customers (ie functional departments) of the outcomes of the selection process, as well as providing individual feedback to the applicants themselves. When designing optimal selection procedures the purpose of each of these functions needs to be borne in mind, as, in part, they serve as standards by which the procedure should be evaluated.

Design cycle model

Roe's (1984, 1989) model (see Figure 5.1) begins with a definition of the problem to be addressed by the organization's selection procedure. For example, an organization may be having difficulties in reducing accident rates and may, in conjunction with other initiatives, wish to address the problem by adapting current selection procedures to ensure that only those applicants with high levels of safety awareness are recruited. In order to do this new selection procedures will have to be developed or existing ones adapted. Before this can be done, however, it will be necessary to identify the particular requirements that the selection procedure must meet. Typically these can be stated as the collection of relevant information, predicting applicants' job performance by evaluating their performance on various selection tests, making selection decisions and providing feedback to all those involved. In the context of the safety example, this will entail identifying and collecting information about the safety knowledge and behaviours required for specific jobs, devising safety-knowledge and work-sample tests, evaluating people's performance on the tests, setting cut-off scores (see Chapter 10) to determine accepts and rejects, and providing feedback to all involved about the efficacy of the procedure.

In addition, the organizational context needs to be analysed to identify and specify any potential constraints. For example, time limits, or a lack of resources for devising or implementing selection tests, may be organizational features that detrimentally impact on the proposed selection procedure. At this stage it may also be worth examining the 'fit' between the proposed selection procedure and the organization's overall selection policies in terms of ethical standards, ethnic-minority selection quotas, equal opportunities, etc.

Once the requirements and constraints have been identified, they need to be synthesized into a preliminary working model of the whole selection procedure. This should specify in writing the technical properties that the procedure should possess (e.g. minimum levels of reliability and criterion-related validity), as well as a description of the overall selection procedure. Ideally, the human resource specialist designing the procedure will possess sufficient knowledge about people and their behaviour, as well as methodological knowledge about various selection tools and techniques.

The next stage is concerned with the testing or simulation of the preliminary selection procedure in terms of its operational, predictive and economic properties. Appropriate questions to ask at this stage may include, for example:

- How long does the procedure take?
- How many applicants can the procedure be used to assess within a certain time period?
- What is the validity and reliability of the selection instruments?
- How effective is the procedure in obtaining information?
- How fair is the procedure?
- What is the benefit/cost ratio?

Once these properties of the procedure are known, they should be evaluated against the previously identified requirements and constraints to ascertain if the preliminary model is satisfactory.

The final stage is concerned with making decisions about whether or not to accept the procedure for operational use. If the procedure is rejected it may be necessary to return to earlier stages so that modifications and improvements can be made. As with the design of most objects or things it should be recognized that the design of an optimal selection procedure may take several attempts. However, the benefits to be gained from a sound selection procedure will tend to outweigh any additional costs attached.

Evaluative standards

Optimizing selection procedures with the design cycle model offers many advantages. The main one is that, as a result of explicitly stating the particular problem and the proposed solutions, the design cycle focuses attention on activities that might otherwise be ignored or at least not be fully considered. For example, designers must give consideration to possible changes in the job, or operational environments over the time period that the selection procedure will be in use. Other advantages reside in the fact that the design cycle explicitly incorporates feedback loops, enabling possible errors in the systems design to be recognized and systematically addressed. Typically, errors in the system's design are recognized when each part of the procedure is evaluated against certain standards, the most important being the effectiveness and efficiency of the procedures, their impact on applicants, and managerial considerations.

The effectiveness of a procedure is usually assessed on the basis of whether or not it yields the right information which leads to the right applicants being chosen. If the right information is not being obtained about either the predictor (e.g. job-knowledge test) or the criterion (e.g. work performance), it may be that different or more thorough data collection methods are needed. Similarly, the effectiveness of the medium used to attract suitably qualified applicants, such as internal advertising, newspapers, professional organizations or recruitment agencies, needs careful consideration, as does the information used to attract applicants in advertisements. A balance needs to be struck between 'selling' the organization to potential applicants via glossy images, and providing realistic job information.

In terms of efficiency standards, each step and instrument used in the design of a selection procedure may add value to the overall procedure's utility, but may also add to the costs involved. Typically, the costs and expected benefits tend to increase at different rates, with utility tending to level off, while costs continue to rise. Thus the benefit/cost ratio is a particularly important standard, and should be monitored. Roe (1989) proposes two main ways of enhancing the cost/utility ratio: reducing the test length, or duration of the procedure to cut costs; and introducing multiple stages into the selection procedure, by, for example, using psychological tests at the beginning of the selection process to sift out applicants prior to the remainder undergoing a selection procedure at an assessment centre. This means that the number of applicants is reduced in stages, leading to further reductions in cost. A case study conducted by Payne et al. (1992) at Ford of Europe showed that this strategy could reduce assessment centre costs from £788.46 to £187.50 per selected candidate. This approach, however, is only likely to be viable when the selection ratio is low (i.e. when there is a large number of candidates).

Other evaluative standards involve ethical considerations. These are mainly concerned with issues surrounding the privacy of applicants so that information about them is not only stored safely but is accurate and available for inspection, and avoiding unfair discriminatory practices (see Chapter 11). Typically this latter issue will revolve around how decisions are made to accept or reject applicants.

Managerial considerations are another important evaluative standard. In practice these considerations are most likely to be concerned with optimizing the use of personnel to reduce the labour costs associated with the overall selection procedure. This might be achieved by standardizing the length of interviews or tests, rescheduling the order of activities to optimize the use of personnel, or conducting more thorough job analyses to satisfy other organizational concerns, in addition to selection needs (e.g. meeting legislative requirements for risk assessments).

The finished design

The final outcomes of the design cycle model may be recorded and incorporated into a two-part user manual that outlines and makes clear which activities should be undertaken at each stage of the selection procedure and by whom. The first part should provide instructions for proper use of the procedure, and could include:

- a description of the facilities required;
- the number and types of staff at each stage;
- administration instructions for the various selection procedures;
- aids such as checklists, norm tables, forms, etc.

The second part should focus on the technical properties of the overall selection procedure, and should include:

- a flow chart of the overall procedure, which specifies the chronological order of activities and the relationships between them;

- descriptions of the data-gathering techniques used to design the procedure;
- the standards applied throughout the design cycle and how they have been met;
- descriptions of the selection methods to be used and decision-making criteria, including data on predictive validity and utility.

The advantages of developing user manuals as described, reside in their applicability in different situations. For example, they can be used in the defence of unfair discrimination litigation; they can provide an objective basis for evaluating selection procedures for different job classes; they allow non-HR personnel, such as line managers, to familiarize themselves with the organization's selection procedures; they can assist in reducing the duplication of effort across sites, plants or facilities; and they can be used to monitor the attenuation of the procedure's validity over a period of time.

SUMMARY

With the utility and design-cycle methodologies described above, human resource specialists are well placed to assess and enhance return on investment. The standards described allow any errors in the design and implementation of selection procedures to be systematically recognized and corrected. This will assist in assuring the quality of both the overall selection procedure and any outcomes, because optimal selection procedures result in the recruitment of better and more productive employees. The main standards that apply are the procedure's effectiveness in providing relevant information, the efficiency of the procedure in enhancing benefit/cost ratios, and the efficacy of the procedure for minimising the possibility of adverse impact on the applicants. The advantages of evaluating a selection procedure according to these standards reside in the focusing of attention on activities and practices that might otherwise not be considered.

6 Selection methods – interviewing

Twelve applicants for the post of marketing coordinator were chosen for interview by a small (200 people) office-furniture manufacturing company. The company, 'Desktop', planned to expand in size over the next two years. A sales manager with previous interviewing experience was given the job of helping the personnel officer to undertake the interviewing of the candidates. It was agreed that each would interview all of the candidates and then they would compare their choices as to who was the best person for the job.

The sales manager began his interviews by inviting the candidate to sit in a chair placed in front of his desk and engaging in small talk, while assessing each applicant's appearance and demeanour. Thereafter the sales manager referred to the candidate's application form and asked questions related to the information previously supplied. He did some checking with questions like 'Do you have a company car at present?' and 'Are you happy working weekends and some evenings?' When it came to questions about previous work experience they tended to be questions like 'You have worked with similar types of people before, haven't you? and 'Have you done similar work to this before?' After these questions the sales manager asked the candidates how they spent their leisure time, ending with a general chat about the government of the day. The candidates were then interviewed by the personnel officer, who invited them to sit with her in some easy chairs, by a coffee table. After small talk, and outlining the procedure that would be followed throughout the interview, she asked all the candidates the same series of 'Tell me about . . .' and 'What would you do if . . .?' type questions.

The personnel officer recorded each candidate's answers on a pre-prepared response sheet based on a previous job analysis, while rating each answer on a scale that indicated whether or not the response was good, average or poor. After completing the questions, candidates were asked if they wanted to add anything further, or ask questions about the job or company. In addition, the personnel officer assessed each candidate's social skills for expressiveness, self-confidence and liveliness using a predetermined scoring guide.

Upon completion of all the interviews, the personnel officer and sales manager ranked their candidates from best to worse. Major differences were found between the rankings. The personnel officer's most preferred candidate was the sales manager's least preferred choice. After some discussion, it became apparent that the sales manager's choices were influenced by impressions of the candidates' appearances and general demeanour, along with their educational qualifications, political views and leisure interests. The personnel officer had focused solely upon the candidates' abilities and their previous work experience.

TRADITIONAL VS STRUCTURED INTERVIEWS

It becomes clear from the Desktop example that not all interviews are the same, and that particular features will influence the quality of the information obtained, which will subsequently affect decisions about whom to select or reject. The most important feature of an interview is the way it is conducted. In the above example, the difference in choice of candidates came about because the sales manager followed the traditional ad hoc interview format which relies heavily on intuitive impressions of the candidate's suitability, and the use of closed or leading questions, requiring little more than 'yes', 'no' or obvious responses. In contrast, the personnel officer used a structured format that focused much more on job-related factors, with open-ended questions that required in-depth answers. The strategy adopted by the personnel officer is supported by the available research evidence, in that structured interviews, utilizing job-related questions, are better predictors of candidates' subsequent performance than interviews with little or no structure. This is probably related to the fact that structural constraints force interviewers to pay more attention to job-related items of information, while minimizing opportunities for collecting irrelevant information, as well as reducing the effects of prejudice and bias on selection decisions.

The usefulness of traditional selection interviews, which typically focus on identifying characteristics of the candidate thought to be important in the job, has been called into question by many reviewers (e.g. Arvey and Campion, 1982), because of their poor predictive power. Typically, their mean validity coefficient (see Chapter 4) is less than +0.2, whereas the mean validity coefficient for structured interviews is in the region of +0.44. Despite this poor predictive power, the traditional ad hoc interview is still widely used in the UK. The reliability and validity of the interview, like that of any other selection method, is of major concern. The relatively poor reliability and validity of the traditional unstructured interview is thought to be associated with the lack of standardization. As demonstrated in the Desktop scenario, this often leads to different interviewers being unable to agree in their assessment of different candidates (inter-judge reliability). Similarly, difficulties arise when interviewers assess the same candidate on more than one occasion (intra-judge reliability). These two issues are central to the reliability of interviews, but the available research suggests, with few exceptions, that the inter-judge reliability of traditional interviewing is low. Intra-judge reliability is often much better, though it may be affected by memory and bias. Accordingly, it makes good commercial sense to improve both the reliability and validity of the interview by providing structure.

Structured interviewing

Good examples of structured, job-related interviews that focus on behaviour are provided by the situational interviewing (SI) approach developed by Gary Latham and colleagues (e.g. Latham and Saari, 1984), the Patterned Behaviour Description Interviewing (PBDI) approach developed by Tom Janz (e.g. Janz, 1989a), and the Multimodal Interviewing method (MMI) developed by Heinz Schuler (e.g. Schuler and Funke, 1989). The multimodal interview combines the best of situational and behavioural interviewing, while also focusing on other important features.

Although similarities between these methods exist, the emphasis of each approach is somewhat different (see Table 6.1 for comparisons). For example, situational interviews focus on an individual's ability to project what his or her future behaviour would be in a given situation. This form of interviewing is grounded in goal-setting theory (Locke and Latham, 1990) and is predicated on the belief that intentions or goals are the immediate precursor of a person's behaviour. Conversely, the PBDI approach is based on the empirical

Table 6.1 Comparisons between structured interview methods

Characteristics	SI	PBDI	MMI
Based on theory	×	—	×
Job analyses: Critical Incidents Technique	×	×	×
Client writes and asks questions	×	—	/
Psychologist/trained interviewer prepares and asks questions	—	×	/
Same questions asked of all applicants	×	—	/
Probing allowed or encouraged	—	×	×
Scoring guide for interviewers	×	—	×
Questions emphasize past	—	×	×
Questions emphasize future	×	—	×
Emphasis is on behaviour	×	×	×
Check for social desirability	×	—	/
Evidence of reliability	×	×	×
Evidence of validity	×	×	×
Evidence of utility	×	×	×
Evidence of test fairness	×	—	/
Evidence of practicality	×	—	×
Assesses other features	—	—	×

Key: × = present; — = not present; / = partial: SI = Situational Interviews; PBDI = Patterned Behaviour Description Interview; MMI = Multimodal Interviewing
Source: Adapted from Latham 1989

truism that 'past behaviour predicts future behaviour'. Candidates are presented with a description of a situation, and asked to explain how they have behaved previously in this or a similar situation. In essence, the major difference in emphasis between the situational and PBDI forms of interviewing can be stated as a focus on 'What would you do IF . . .?' versus 'What did you do WHEN . . .?' type questions. For example, a situational interviewer might ask an applicant, 'What would you do if your spouse was away visiting and your child became ill a couple of hours before you were due to start work?', whereas a PBDI interviewer might say, 'Tell me about the last time you had to miss work and stay at home. What was the reason? What did you do?' The emphasis of the MMI approach is one that focuses on both the past and the future by using both situational and biographical questions, while also providing the opportunity to assess different psychological constructs such as an applicant's social competence or achievement motivation.

Notably, all three approaches focus on examples of behaviour derived from job analyses, rather than attitudinal or personality variables. Nonetheless, one practical disadvantage of a focus on past behaviour is that inexperienced applicants (e.g. graduates) may not be able to respond in a meaningful way, which suggests that situational or multimodal interviews, focusing on future intentions may be more appropriate to use with these groups of people. The PBDI approach is based on the assumption that applicants are very self-aware, that memory is unaffected or that bias will not be introduced, none of which is necessarily the case.

Other differences relate to the composition of the interviews. For example, the PBDI approach encourages in-depth probing, with the responses rated according to subjective interviewer judgements, whereas situational interviews require responses only to specific questions that are recorded according to predetermined benchmark answers, rated as good, average or poor. In contrast, multimodal interviewing is more versatile, because it explicitly incorporates various dimensions within an interview session, each of which are scored on behaviourally anchored rating scales. For example, candidates are assessed on self-presentation skills, vocational interests and organizational choice, a separate free-ranging conversation period where interviewers can probe the candidate, and specific biographical and situational questions where no probing takes place. In addition, the MMI can be adapted to assess other applicant features thought to be important. These might include an assessment of the candidate's social competence or achievement motivation. Moreover, unlike the other two approaches, multimodal interviewing specifically incorporates a realistic job preview whereby information is provided that tells applicants what the job is really like, the lifestyle involved, the prevailing organizational culture, etc. This feature, in particular, is likely to enhance the benefit/cost ratios of the overall selection procedure by reducing organizational turnover. Research reveals that realistic job previews tend to lower initial job expectations, while increasing self-selection, organizational commitment, job satisfaction, job performance and job survival.

Developing structured interviews

Each of the above approaches begins with a thorough analysis of the job to identify examples of particularly good or poor performance in the job (see Chapter 3). These examples are then rated by job experts or job holders to provide benchmarks for interviewers to use when scoring the responses of interviewees. Subsequently, an item bank of situational questions is developed along with a behaviourally based scoring key for each question (e.g. poor, average, good). This key provides a systematic scoring procedure, which helps to maximize both the reliability and the validity of judgements about candidates. When these scoring guides are not used, structured interviews are often no better than unstructured interviews. Some researchers have developed scales based on the procedure for behaviourally anchored rating scales (BARS, see Chapter 3). Whichever procedure is used, it is important to ensure that the consistency and objectivity of subsequent scoring is monitored by frequent inter-rater reliability checks. Once the materials have been developed, interviewers are then trained in observation, interpersonal skills, judgemental skills, interview conduct and question formulation. Subsequently, interviewers are given practice with the interview questions and provided with performance feedback. The use of video cameras may be appropriate here to facilitate feedback.

During the interview itself, twelve or so questions chosen from the previously developed item bank are administered one at a time (either orally or on cards) to each candidate. Ensuring that each candidate is asked the same questions is an important feature of structured interviews identified by Campion et al. (1988). However, other researchers suggest that candidates can be asked standardized questions, from a predetermined set of categories, rather than identical questions. An example of a question and scoring key taken from a study by Robertson et al. (1990) is as follows.

An example of a situational interview item

Two young people in their early 20s have approached the organization for finance to set up a new venture making and selling equipment to enable home computer users to translate games easily between different models of computers. They are enthusiastic and talented, but freely confess that they have no business, manufacturing or selling experience. What advice will you give them?

Scale points

Low	Contact someone else (e.g. accountant) for information on cash flows
	Tell them not to go ahead, too risky, no market
Medium	Recommend information to them
	Tell them to recruit business person
	Tell them accountant will prepare cost report
	Arrange for them to see organization's experts
	Ask them to talk more once they have thought some more about their business proposition
High	Say the organization is enthusiastic about them as customers
	Ask them about legal side of game translation
	Do they have a prototype?
	Contact Patent Office
	Seems a big area of growth at the moment
	Obtain information and recommend: Board of Trade, new businesses, offer organization's own information, accountants

In essence, three features common to structured interviewing are important: questions should be developed on the basis of job analyses, every candidate should be asked the same type of questions, and a systematic scoring procedure should be used.

Evaluative standards

In recent years, structured interviews have generally produced good validity data. Impressive validities have been reported for multimodal interviewing, across a range of occupations encompassing banking apprentices, business students – four and a half years after interview – and industrial Research & Development scientists and engineers. *Uncorrected* predictive validity coefficients ranged from 0.27 to 0.37. In a review of the validity of four multimodal interviewing studies, Schuler and Moser (1995) reported a *corrected* validity for the R & D study at 0.51. Interestingly, other recent research suggests that situational interviews that focus on future intentions lead to better criterion-related validity (0.50) than PBDI interviews which emphasize past behaviours (0.39) (McDaniel et al., 1994). This may reflect the theoretical underpinning of each approach. These order-of-magnitude differences in validity could make a significant difference to estimates of financial gain using benefit/cost ratios (see Chapter 5). Research also revealed that the criterion-related validity of structured interviews is better for individual interviews than for panel interviews (0.46 vs 0.38). In comparison with individual interviews, panel interviews are more costly, time-consuming and difficult to arrange, and even though they ought to be more reliable, because more than one person provides ratings of each applicant, inter-judge reliability is usually low. Taken together, the implications of this body of research are that structured multimodal or situational interviews using behaviourally based scoring guides with one interviewer are more reliable, valid and cost-effective. From the authors' knowledge, this view is beginning to gain credence as many consulting firms and human resource professionals are beginning to focus on job-related behaviours during structured interviews, although there is continued use of interview panels.

The reliability of structured interviews has been found to be much higher than the traditional interview, mainly due to the use of behaviourally based scoring guides. This was demonstrated in a situational-interview study conducted by Latham and Saari (1984). They reported that the interviewers had initially recorded their overall impressions of each applicant rather than using the scoring guide. Subsequent reassessments of the same applicants using the scoring guide produced much better reliability and validity data. In general, all three types of structured interviews exhibit acceptable inter-observer reliability (0.71 to 0.96) and internal consistency (0.61 to 0.82) data.

A very positive attribute of structured interviews is the likelihood of 'freedom from bias' due to rating errors such as 'similar to me', first impressions and leniency effects. In addition, they are much less likely to discriminate unfairly between applicants on the basis of race or sex, and, as such, they are less difficult to defend in litigation suits. This evidence suggests that structured interviews are more consistent with the UK Equal Opportunities Commission's Code of Practice, which states that 'questions posed during interviews should relate *only* to the requirements of the job. Where it is necessary to discuss personal circumstances, and their effect upon ability to do the job, this should be done in a neutral manner, equally applicable to all applicants.'

The acceptability of structured interviews appears to be another strikingly positive attribute. Research conducted in the USA compared the practicality of traditional interviews with structured interviews as perceived by users, employees, potential applicants and lawyers. Users included senior executives, line managers and HR personnel. The results indicated that the user group preferred structured interviews because they allowed them to:

- appear organized and prepared;
- determine the ability of applicants to do the job;
- compare applicants on an objective basis;
- hire/reject applicants solely on job-related reasons.

Structured interviews received a lower rating for ease of preparation, because they typically take at least one day to prepare, unlike ad hoc interviews which can be done on the spur of the moment. Many employees did not view one form as preferable to the other, but college students expressed a preference for traditional interviews as they were more likely to win lawsuits for unfair discrimination. As would be expected, lawyers preferred structured interviews because they were the easiest to defend against accusations of unfair discrimination against rejected candidates. The reasons cited were that:

- they are based on job analyses;
- the questions are representative of actual job-related behaviour;
- they are less prone to interviewer bias;
- all applicants are asked the same questions.

Although, this research was conducted in the USA, the findings are unlikely to differ significantly from the UK, judging by structured interviews' increasing popularity.

In terms of utility, Campion et al. (1988) estimated a figure of $100,000 per annum with the use of situational interviews with 149 candidates who were hired. Similarly, Schuler et al. (in press) conducted a utility analysis for the R & D study assessment centre as a whole, of which multimodal interviewing formed a part. Somewhat surprisingly, the multimodal interview yielded a validity coefficient comparable to the whole assessment centre. This suggests that the potential pay-offs from multimodal interviewing alone are equal to those from assessment centres.

INTERVIEWS AS SOCIAL INTERACTIONS

It is important to recognize that interviewing is essentially an interactive social process. As such it is subject to potential problems due to faulty communications and judgements by both interviewer and candidate. These problems are likely to be particularly relevant to traditional unstructured interviews. In 1981, using attribution theory as a framework (see Kelley and Michela, 1980), Herriot argued that the commonly observed low validities of the traditional employment interview may, in part, be due to misunderstandings between the parties regarding their respective roles, and/or interviewers misinterpreting candidates' behaviour.

The root of most of these potential problems appears to reside in the different expectations that each party holds of the other. This may be further compounded by either party committing what is referred to as 'the fundamental attribution error' (see Chapter 10) by attributing too much of the cause of the others' behaviour to personal factors, without regard to the influence of situational factors. For example, interviewers will tend to believe that candidates who appear anxious during the interview are behaving anxiously because they are anxious people, rather than because they are in a stressful interview. A good example of the mismatch between interviewer and candidate expectations, and the influence this has on hiring decisions, is provided by Herriot and Rothwell's (1981) study of real-life interviews, which demonstrated that interviewers expected the candidates to spend more time talking about themselves, whereas candidates expected interviewers to spend more time talking about the job and the organization. The less candidates talked about themselves and asked questions of the interviewer, the less likely they were seen as suitable for the job. This latter point highlights the fact that the way people are viewed is partly a function of their 'in-role' or 'out-of-role' behaviour. A person exhibiting in-role behaviour is usually following the norms dictated by the prevailing circumstances, whereas someone exhibiting out-of-role behaviour is usually seen as following his or her own personal preferences. Very often, however, the rules to be followed during an interview are neither clear nor universally held, which can lead to either party perceiving the other as a rule breaker, resulting in unfavourable attributions.

These in-role or out-of-role behaviours may also extend to verbal behaviour (e.g. what is said), non-verbal behaviour (e.g body language), articulative behaviour (e.g. loudness of voice, fluency of speech, etc), and appearance (e.g. dress). All of these behaviours can influence subsequent accept/reject decisions by the organization and/ or the candidate. Investigations of the influence of verbal, non-verbal and articulative behaviours on selection decisions in real-life interviews have revealed that 'what is said' has the most influence on accept/reject decisions, followed closely by how articulate the candidate is. The candidate's composure and personal appearance are also important, but not to the same extent. Eye contact also exerts a powerful influence on accept/reject decisions. Rejected candidates tend to be those who avoid eye contact, smile less and are tense. Conversely, successful candidates tend to be those who display higher levels of eye contact. In 1990, Neil Anderson and Viv Shackleton found that interviewers' impressions of a candidate's personality were influenced by the candidate's non-verbal behaviour, in terms of eye contact, facial expressions, hand gestures, head movements and posture. These impressions of a candidate's personality subsequently influenced accept/reject decisions. They also found that the degree to which interviewers personally liked the candidate and the degree to which the interviewer and candidate were seen as alike also influenced hiring decisions. Similarly, other research has shown that the more attractive the candidate is in the interviewer's eyes, the greater the likelihood of a job offer. As a whole, the above evidence suggests that the amount of eye contact, which is viewed as a reflection of the candidate's self-confidence, plays a very important role during interviews. There is, however, an internal contradiction. On the one hand, interviewers appear to expect candidates to maintain high levels of eye contact. On the other hand, interviewers expect candidates to do the majority of the talking. Candidates who do not maintain high levels of eye contact are seen as exhibiting out-of-role behaviours. In fact, what they are doing is perfectly appropriate and in-role, because, on average, listeners look at speakers 75 percent of the time, whereas speakers look at listeners only 40 percent of the time. This means that a candidate who talks much of the time cannot be expected to also retain high levels of eye contact with the interviewer(s). This is a prime example of false expectations on the part of interviewers that can result in negative attributions about the candidate.

Some research has also been undertaken to assess the effects of candidates' perceptions of interviewers. It has been found that the interviewer's communication style (eye contact, head nods and smiling) affects both the candidate's perceptions of the interviewer and the interviewer's own performance. Similarly, when interviewers do not maintain eye contact, candidates' responses to questions tend to be shorter. In turn this adversely affects the likelihood of being offered a job. Schmitt and Coyle (1976) found that candidates' perceptions of the interviewers' personality and non-verbal behaviour influenced their decisions to accept or reject job offers. More recently, it was found that the degree to which an interviewer is believed to listen influenced candidates' willingness to accept job offers. Similarly, interviewer characteristics such as personableness, competency and informativeness influence candidates' perceptions of the job and impressions of the organization, which in turn affect candidates' decisions to accept a job offer. Although not exhaustive, the above evidence is important, because it demonstrates the ways in which interviewers and applicants simultaneously react to each other, influencing both hiring decisions and candidates' decisions to accept job offers.

INFLUENCES ON INTERVIEW DECISION-MAKING

Other factors related to the interviewing process are also thought to influence hire or reject decisions. Some evidence suggests that interviewers place more weight on negative rather than positive information about candidates (see Chapter 10). During the late 1950s it was suggested that interviewers actively sought negative information about candidates, in order to confirm initial impressions made during the first four minutes of the interview. Several studies undertaken during the 1960s and 1970s supported this notion, suggesting that negative information was weighted approximately twice as heavily as positive information. In recent years this view has not been consistently supported. Studies conducted during the 1980s have found that, regardless of initial impressions, interviewers prefer to seek positive information from candidates. However, some research suggests that less suitable candidates are asked more negative questions. This might be because interviewers are more concerned to avoid hiring a poor candidate than they are about rejecting a good one, particularly if they are held accountable for their decisions. Indeed, some evidence suggests that the more interviewers are held accountable for selection decisions the more likely they are to base decisions on stereotypical views of their ideal candidate.

Because many interviews result in subjective judgements, they are particularly prone to the introduction of bias, which may also affect subsequent hiring decisions. In terms of bias, clear evidence has been found that women with exactly the same credentials as men get fewer job offers, although this is moderated by the type of job applied for. In general, people have quite firmly held stereotypical views about whether jobs are 'male', 'female' or neutral. Managerial work and truck-driving are more often than not seen as jobs for men, whereas beauticians and secretaries are generally seen as female roles. A candidate's suitability for a job can also be predicted from how attractive interviewers think they are. Attractive women applying for clerical jobs tend to obtain more positive evaluations than less attractive women, whereas attractive women applying for managerial jobs are rated more negatively than less attractive women. Even when women applicants represent less than a quarter of the applicant pool, they are still viewed less favourably. Some evidence also suggests that racial biases may be introduced in the interview process because of the stereotypical views interviewers have of ethnic minority personalities and background (see Jenkins, 1986). Similarly, a limited amount of evidence suggests that disabled candidates are usually credited with high levels of motivation, but they are also less likely to be offered a job. Candidates who have experienced nervous breakdowns are also not favoured when it comes to selection decisions.

INTERVIEWER TRAINING

Many organizations assume that one way to become an effective interviewer is through experience. However, research evidence suggests that experienced interviewers tend not to agree with each other, just as do less experienced interviewers. This may be because the conditions necessary for learning are not present during the interview. Training interviewers is one way to attempt to reduce bias, with a resulting increase in reliability and validity.

The evidence relating to the training of interviewers is, however, somewhat mixed. Training can focus on the reduction of errors when ratings are given. Nonetheless, although this kind of training does reduce errors, particularly if practice and feedback is used, training in the use of structured interviewing techniques appears to be far more effective. For example, one of the authors (Robertson et al., 1990) provided situational interview training to interviewers in a financial services organization, who were assessing internal candidates for promotion. This training encompassed two distinct phases, the first of which focused on the aims of the process and how to interview, while the second consisted of a number of practice role-play sessions. In addition, behavioural models of a video-taped situational interview were used to demonstrate the target behaviour. Evidence collected 18 months after the interviews indicated that the average interview scores given by raters correlated with the candidates' subsequent performance scores.

Training focused more on improving interviewer behaviour than on the reduction of rating errors, is useful. For example, using behavioural evaluation methodology on a five-day interview training course, Howard and his colleagues (e.g. Howard and Dailey, 1979) found training to be extremely effective, even though the people already had interviewing experience. The training focused on the improvement of the trainees' questioning techniques, structuring of the interview, providing support, establishing rapport, listening skills and attention to relevant material, with a mixture of practice, discussion, demonstration and feedback. The above evidence suggests that, without training, interviewers tend to see candidates differently, but with training many differences can be minimized, resulting in increased reliability and validity. The effectiveness of training may reside in the encouragement of interviewers to follow optimum procedures, with the result that the opportunity for bias and prejudice diminishes.

SUMMARY

Structured interviews are much better than traditional ad hoc interviews because they are more focused on job-related features derived from job analyses. This means that interviewers know what questions to ask and why they are asking them. Because every applicant is rated more objectively, the inadvertent introduction of bias and unfairness is also minimized. In addition, structured interviews are more likely to meet the necessary evaluative standards of reliability, validity and practicality. As such they will tend to deliver quality people who meet job demands the first time around.

7 Selection methods – sample based

During the latter part of the 1980s, 'Wheels', a large engineering company manufacturing car components and accessories, had taken note of the projected labour shortages forecast for the following decades. To ensure that they would have sufficient numbers of skilled personnel to take the company forward over the 1990s, they adopted a policy of annually providing thirty training places in engineering to school leavers. In the interim period, due to the projected retirement of ageing workers, they decided to recruit smaller numbers of skilled personnel, as and when required, to ensure continuity of production. The company's intention was to recruit only trainees after the first batch had completed their training.

In view of the costs involved in providing five-year apprenticeships, the human resource officer was given the task of devising tests which would identify suitable individuals with the potential for undertaking long-term training that would involve both theory and practice. The HR officer visited a 'Skillcentre' run by the Manpower Services Commission, to investigate their selection procedures for trainees. She was particularly impressed with the way they assessed an applicant's ability to learn a new skill, with 'trainability tests', in which applicants were trained to perform a sample of tasks and were then immediately assessed on how well they performed the sample of tasks. She was struck by the simplicity and direct relevance of the tests. Already familiar with the use of work-sample tests to assess experienced personnel, she could see the potential value of work-sample and trainability tests for selecting both skilled and unskilled personnel. She consulted with the resident occupational psychologist who had helped to devise both types of tests. The human resource officer's main concerns were related to how valid and reliable the tests were in predicting people's future performance, and how costly they would be to devise. She was assured that both work-sample and trainability tests were amongst the best selection methods currently available for predicting performance, and that the initial development costs could pay for themselves many times over, particularly in the light of the engineering company's apprenticeship policy.

With the benefit of this information, she consulted the Register of Chartered Psychologists held in the local public library. A consultant occupational psychologist was contracted to devise trainability tests for the apprenticeship scheme and work-sample tests for selecting skilled workers. The psychologist followed a standard five-stage procedure (described later in this chapter), which involved job analyses and interviews with existing training instructors and supervisors to develop both the trainability and work-sample tests and the scoring criteria. After the initial screening of applicants, the tests were administered to eighty potential trainees in groups of two or three. It was found that after taking the tests, some applicants voluntarily dropped out of the process, on the grounds that they did not like the type of work. The remaining applicants were rank-ordered by their test scores. Of these, the thirty highest scoring applicants were offered apprenticeships with the company. Thereafter, the annual 'cadres' of trainees were selected on the basis of trainability tests.

WORK-SAMPLE TESTS

The Wheels example shows that work-sample tests provide a realistic alternative to the 'psychometric testing' approach to personnel selection. There are two fundamental forms of work-sample tests. First, there are the work-sample tests administered to experienced candidates that tap into the skills base required in particular jobs. Second, there are 'trainability' work-sample tests suitable for candidates who have no experience related to the job applied for. Essentially, these types of test are based upon the premise that 'past behaviour is the best predictor of future behaviour'. Asher and Sciarrino (1974) in their review of work-sample tests made a very powerful argument for point-to-point correspondence between predictors and criteria on the basis that 'like predicts like'. In other words, they argued that the behaviours used as predictors, and the conditions in which they are tested, should be as similar as possible to the actual work behaviour required in the job (criteria).

The efficacy of the work-sample testing approach to selection is aptly demonstrated in a comparative study between a work-sample test and a battery of paper-and-pencil aptitude tests (Campion, 1972). A work-sample test for maintenance mechanics was devised on the basis of job analyses. Performance on four particular tasks was deemed to discriminate between good and poor workers. These tasks reflected the ability of mechanics to install pulleys and belts; disassemble and repair a gear box; install and correctly align a motor; press a bush into a sprocket and ream it to fit onto a shaft. The validity of the work-sample test was subsequently assessed with supervisory ratings of each applicant's ability in the use of tools, the accuracy of work and overall mechanical ability. Comparisons were made between applicants' scores on the work-sample tests and on psychometric aptitude tests for predicting performance. The results showed that the work-sample test was better at predicting performance than the aptitude tests.

Two main types of work-sample tests can be identified: motor and verbal. 'Motor' tests refer to physical manipulations (e.g. bricklaying, sewing, operating lathes, etc.), and 'verbal' tests refer to language- or people-oriented tasks (e.g. problem-solving exercises). Robertson and Kandola (1982) widened the scope of work-samples when they suggested the following four-category system.

1   *Psychomotor*, which involves the physical manipulation of objects;

2   *Job-related information*, which examines the extent of an applicant's existing job knowledge;

3   *Individual/situational decision-making*, where an applicant's ability to make decisions similar to those found in the job is examined with in-tray exercises or hypothetical situations;

4   *Group discussions/decision-making*, where groups of applicants are put together to discuss particular topics and each individual's performance is assessed on the basis of his or her contribution. Typically, this form is used almost entirely for assessing managerial potential.

Many examples of work-sample tests are in the scientific literature. They include manual, clerical, administrative, supervisory and managerial tests, although the majority are devoted to psychomotor tests. An example of a clerical work-sample test (developed by the occupational psychologists, Pearn Kandola) is given in Table 7.1.

Job-knowledge tests

In their strictest sense, job-knowledge tests are not 'pure' work-sample tests, because they examine the amount of job-related information that a candidate holds, but do not actually require candidates to demonstrate job-related behaviours. Nonetheless, these tests examine at least two types of critical job knowledge: the required technical 'know-how' to perform a job, and knowledge of the processes and judgemental criteria required for effective performance in a job. The reason job-knowledge tests can be used as surrogate work-sample tests is because of the major role job knowledge plays in linking job performance with an applicant's ability and experience. However, it is necessary for the job-knowledge tests to be job-specific, even within a particular class of job. For example, a welder in a shipyard will be likely to use different equipment and processes from a welder in an engineering workshop. One particular advantage of job-knowledge tests is that they can also be used to assess important secondary features of jobs as they can furnish useful developmental information which provides a base for selection decisions and subsequent training. They are ideal, for example, to ascertain an applicant's levels of safety awareness and

Source: Courtesy of Pearn Kandola

Table 7.1 A clerical work-sample test

Executive Officers often have to complete statistical returns and this section tests your ability to do that.

You will be presented with tables of data with some information missing. By using other details in the table you will be able to calculate the missing information.

The example below is taken from an analysis of job leavers broken down by ethnic group, gender and reasons for leaving. The table has three empty boxes which need completing.

| Ethnic Group | Reason for leaving | | | D Total leavers | Job entry rate as a % (A ÷ D) 1 × 100 | TI final output rate as a % ([A + B] ÷ D) × 100 |
	A Job	B Other final output	C Other			
I	23	2	1	26	88.5	96.2
II	(1)	1	0	15	93.3	100.0
III	14	3	2	19	(2)	89.5
Total	51	6	3	60	85.0	95.0
Male	23	3	1	27	85.2	96.3
Female	28	3	2	33	84.9	(3)
Total	51	6	3	60	85.0	95.0

Source: Courtesy of Pearn Kandola

specific knowledge, prior to selection, where safety is an important feature of an organization's functioning.

Trainability tests

Unlike 'pure' work-sample tests for experienced candidates, the main purpose of trainability work-sample tests is to assess whether inexperienced applicants are suitable for training or not. The essential difference between trainability tests and work-sample tests is that trainability tests involve structured and controlled learning periods. Instructors demonstrate the task while giving standardized instructions during which applicants are encouraged to ask questions. Applicants then attempt the task and, with the aid of a checklist, the trainee's efforts are assessed in terms of how things are done (e.g. the number of errors) as well as what is done (i.e. the finished product). Typically, applicants also assess their own performance and tend to select themselves in or out of jobs based on self-assessment, suggesting that these tests provide a realistic job preview. A good example of this is reported in a study by Cascio and Phillips (1979) where applicants for sewer mechanics withdrew after being tested in an underground sewage chamber. Trainability tests have been developed for several occupational areas and have produced consistently good validity data (Robertson and Downs, 1989). The first research on trainability tests was conducted in UK government training centres in 1968 by Sylvia Downs to assess the suitability of older workers for training as welders and carpenters. Subsequently, tests were developed in industry to help select sewing machinists, electronics assemblers and construction workers. Tests have also been developed for engineering, forestry, catering, dentistry and helicopter navigation, in addition to certain supervisory and managerial positions (Downs, 1985).

Developing trainability tests

The development of trainability tests is a fairly straightforward and robust procedure. Job analyses (see Chapter 3) are used to derive the behavioural elements of the test. The main focus of attention, however, is on errors that normally occur in training and on the job. It is essential to derive specific descriptions of errors. The specific behavioural aspects of the job that distinguish between good and poor performance need to be identified. These should be double-checked with instructors and supervisors, in order to clarify and clear up any misunderstandings. The more the behavioural aspects distinguish between good and poor performance, the more likely that test validity will be high. The specific checklist items are written so that they are negatively worded, and then compiled into an error checklist that represents the job as closely as possible, while also incorporating varying levels of difficulty. The sequence of errors on the checklist should correspond to the order in which errors are likely to occur during the task. Similarly, any errors likely to be present in the finished product (if there is one) should be specified. An overall rating of the trainee's potential is also provided. This might be a simple five-point scale from 'extremely good' to 'would not be trainable'. Each point on the scale would be accompanied by a descriptive rating (e.g. 'C: good enough for simple work, the trainee would be expected to become a steady worker on simple tasks'). The final stage in developing trainability tests is the construction of a detailed training script for use by instructors. In order to standardize the training for each applicant, the script should be written in simple, clear, unambiguous terms and contain all the necessary information for the applicant to perform the task for themselves. From the instructor's point of view, it is better if these scripts reflect the training style and methods already used in the organization.

Advantages and disadvantages of work-sample tests

There are many advantages of work-samples. From the organization's perspective, because they are work-specific they provide a check on the proficiency and competence of applicants in the job prior to engagement. They have also consistently provided good criterion-related validity data (see Hunter and Hunter, 1984). From the applicants' perspective, they act as a realistic job preview and provide applicants with the opportunity to self-select themselves in or out of the selection process. In addition, the tests have high 'face validity' with applicants, and are unlikely to be biased since the opportunity for bias is minimized as the tests focus on what applicants can or cannot do.

Nonetheless, a major problem with these types of tests is that, because they are job-specific, a test suitable for one trade may not necessarily be used even for other closely related trades. For example, one cook's job is likely to be different from other cooks' jobs. Thus, each test must be validated individually, since there is no guarantee that the work-sample chosen will provide a suitable basis for making assessments of future performance in that trade. Equally, it is important to ensure that the tests reflect changes in jobs, as the validity of trainability tests tends to diminish over a period of time. In other words, the longer the follow-up period involved in the validation study, the smaller the resulting validity coefficient. This decrease in validity may be because trainability tests, like all work-sample tests, are closely tied to the specific tasks of the job. As time passes, these job-specific facets of performance may become less important.

Other disadvantages relate to the costs involved in providing the resources required to administer the tests. A bricklaying work-sample test, by necessity, will require facilities (space to build walls etc.), special equipment (e.g. a cement mixer, bricks, tools and protective clothing), and trained instructors, who in the normal course of events are likely to be active in production. This will apply to all work-sample tests, and the more complex they are the more specialist equipment will be required. The choice of whether or not to use work-sample tests should be made on the basis of the balance between the perceived benefits and drawbacks. However, when developing any type of work-sample test it is very important to ensure that the tasks chosen for the test are representative of the required job performance, or else their predictive value may be substantially diminished and may lead to low validity coefficients. Another issue of practical concern is the extent to which trainability tests, which are costly and time-consuming, measure something unique that cannot be assessed more cost-effectively by the use of cognitive tests.

Assessment centres

Assessment centres seem to be an increasingly popular method of selection and assessment in organizational settings. Some 60 per cent of British companies surveyed by Shackleton and Newell in 1991 reported their use, compared to 20 per cent reported by Robertson and Makin in 1986. As well as being used to choose between external candidates, assessment centres are often also used in internal promotion/assessment schemes. The increased popularity of assessment centres is probably related to the fact that in this approach multiple methods of assessment and multiple assessors are used to provide a reasonably objective all-round view of the candidate, which, perhaps, is not possible in the normal course of events. The use of multiple methods and assessors underscores the point that the term 'assessment centre' (AC) is used to describe a *selection process*, rather than a fixed geographical location.

In essence, the AC approach utilizes all the main selection methods (e.g. work-sample tests, structured interviews, and 'paper-and-pencil' tests of mental abilities, aptitudes and personality) in a comprehensive and integrated manner, culminating in a written report for each candidate that usually provides an overall assessment rating (OAR). In combination, multiple methods are thought to lead to more accurate predictions about a candidate's future job performance. As well as being used for selection or promotion decisions, assessment centres may be used for developmental purposes. Developmental assessment centres identify employees' strengths and weaknesses, which enables feedback to be given to both the individual and the employing organization, and usually results in recommendations for training or career counselling, etc.

Candidates are generally assessed in groups of six to eight, by groups of senior managers and/or psychologists over two to three days, although sometimes it may be as little as one day, or as long as a week. The idea behind evaluations' lasting several days is that it is more difficult for candidates to 'bluff' or 'put on a front'. It is fairly easy to describe oneself as 'persuasive' or 'dominant' in a 'paper-and-pencil' test or during interviews, but it is something else to demonstrate these behaviours during challenging exercises with other candidates. Similarly, as the latter point illustrates, group assessments offer distinct advantages in that candidates are assessed within the context of group dynamics, allowing other aspects of each candidate's performance to be monitored.

Typically, ACs are used to identify a candidate's managerial potential, which perhaps reflects the historical roots of the approach in identifying potential military officers or senior civil servants. In fact, assessment centres are also useful for non-managerial jobs. Assessment centres differ in the number of dimensions on which candidates are evaluated (see Table 7.2). Some use about four, others may use more than twenty. The American Telephone & Telegraph Company (AT&T), whose influence on the design of ACs has been considerable, for example, derived twenty-five dimensions on the basis of a literature review and judgements of personnel staff, although not every dimensions is always used. To select students for

Table 7.2 Exercises and dimensions in a typical assessment centre

Dimension	Personality inventory	In-tray exercise	Group discussion	Interview	Presentation
Interpersonal sensitivity	✓		✓	✓	
Problem-solving and analysis		✓	✓		✓
Resilience	✓			✓	
Business skills		✓			✓

sponsorship on university engineering degree courses, with a view to eventual employment, Ford of Europe uses four dimensions concerned with business awareness (knowledge of the industry), interactive awareness (social skills), work structure (organization and planning abilities), and drive and enthusiasm (energy levels). To aid organizations in the choice of dimensions to use when developing assessment centres, published catalogues are available (Development Dimensions, 1975), as well as criteria that might be helpful for rating candidates (Jeswald, 1977). There are also various generic competency frameworks (e.g. Dulewicz, 1989; See Chapter 2).

The key feature common to all modern ACs, however, is their use of simulated tasks to provide a structure by which job-related behaviour can be observed. Schmitt and Ostroff (1986), for example, devised a simulated task for emergency telephone operators in police stations. Candidates were required to 'role-play' an operator, while taking calls from a member of the public (a trained stooge working from a script). Candidates needed to ask a variety of questions to elicit and record the necessary information to send help to the caller. They were allowed one practice trial to familiarize themselves with the procedure. Thereafter, candidates were assessed on the way in which they dealt with the calls. To ensure that the exercise was sufficiently challenging some of the calls were very emotional and hysterical. The various dimensions of assessments in the test included interpersonal, analytical and communication skills, as well as competencies related to operating a switchboard.

In-tray exercises

Simulated managerial tasks (e.g. in-tray and group decision-making exercises) are specifically designed to elicit information about a candidate's leadership, communication (verbal and written), planning and problem-solving skills. Often these simulations require applicants to make decisions under fairly extreme time pressures. Assessors observe the candidates' performance and make judgements about their performance on several dimensions (e.g. supervisory skills, planning/administration, etc.). The ubiquitous in-tray exercise is the most common form of this type of simulated test, particularly for managerial and administrative jobs, as the content can easily be varied to suit the job. Typically, the applicant is provided with a basket or file containing letters, memos and other written material and instructed to act to resolve particular problems.

Several shortcomings have been noted for in-tray exercises. For example, using two different forms of in-tray exercises to measure the same managerial performance dimensions, Brannick et al. (1989) found rather poor correlations between them. This result called into question the validity of inferences (see Chapter 4) derived from the exercises about managerial traits. Similarly, the situational conditions under which these tests are completed are normally very different from real-life situations. In the workplace, many day-to-day decisions are conveyed orally to others, whereas the in-tray exercise usually requires written rather than oral responses. This may well affect subsequent validation attempts. In a concurrent validity study designed to overcome this particular shortcoming, a 30-minute 'role-play' test was developed for telemarketing salespeople (Squires et al., 1991). Candidates were assessed on two incoming telephone calls and two outgoing calls, where the objective was to sell a service contract for an appliance to customers. The assessments focused on four aspects of performance: customer service, administrative efficiency, sales skills and sales results. Independent evaluations of the candidates' performance were found to correlate significantly with both subjective and objective measures of sales performance. When the exercise was conducted in an operational setting with 128 applicants, test scores were highly correlated with subsequent performance, indicating the test's criterion-related validity. As a general principle, in-tray exercises should not only record both verbal and written responses, but every attempt should be made to make the situational conditions as realistic as possible.

Group discussions

Group discussions appear to be an integral part of assessment centres as they are extensively used. Many group-discussion exercises are aimed at assessing managerial potential by providing evidence about applicants' abilities to:

- get on with others;
- influence others;
- express themselves verbally;
- think clearly and logically;
- apply their experience to new problems.

Observers, usually two or three, evaluate and rate participants on a number of dimensions designed to examine features such as leadership potential, interpersonal skills, problem-solving and business awareness. Assigned exercises typically present each participant with the same problem. Participants need to engage in a mixture of competition and collaboration to solve the problem. Ford's student sponsorship AC, for example, asks each applicant to promote an advertising strategy and slogan for the scheme. Similarly, one version used at Shell International Petroleum Company involves a role-play exercise of a newspaper editorial committee. Each candidate has to push a particular news item for the main headline of the following day's publication. Other forms of leaderless group discussions assess applicants' teamwork abilities. These usually involve a group task such as a simulated business game, where applicants have to operate under constantly changing conditions, and are designed to reflect 'real-life' practices that occur in the organization. Evaluations are made of the candidate's overall contribution to the effective functioning of the team, rather than success at promoting a particular product or viewpoint. Nonetheless, not every group discussion is leaderless. The Civil Service Selection Board, for example, requires candidates to take turns to chair 15-minute sessions to obtain agreements as to how to solve a managerial problem of some sort. Similarly, the Admiralty Interview Board of the Royal Navy requires applicants to undertake outdoor command exercises to achieve some objective (e.g. build a bridge over water) to assess leadership potential. In essence, therefore, each different type of group discussion provides a structure within which job-related behaviour can be observed and evaluated. It is important, however, that the content of group discussions be chosen with some care to ensure that specialist knowledge favouring one or two individuals is not introduced. Equally, the exercises should reflect real job situations that correspond to the level of the job. This aspect is frequently overlooked, as designers typically tend to make the exercises either too difficult or too easy.

How applicants' performance is evaluated may also have a bearing on the reliability and validity of these exercises. Observer evaluations may be highly structured in some ACs (e.g. 'gives opinions', 'asks for suggestions'), whereas others may be less structured (e.g. does the applicant appear to influence the thinking of others?). Inevitably, the highly structured approach to evaluations will be more reliable and valid, particularly if behaviourally anchored rating scales are used as the basis for scoring. It is known, for example, that problems exist related to the negative impact of social influences on consensus discussions when assessors pool their judgements (a common procedure). If social pressure is used to cause assessors to adjust their ratings, rather than agree on the true scores, not only will inter-rater reliability estimates be inflated but the appropriate person for the job might not be selected. It makes sense, therefore, to ensure that assessors minimize this possibility by adopting the structured approach.

Developing an assessment centre

In line with most other selection methods, AC exercises should be developed from a thorough job analysis of the job in question (see Chapter 3). This analysis needs to provide a good description of the tasks and situations typically found, so that 'realistic' simulated exercises can be developed. Ideally, these exercises should not only reflect the more important features of the job, but should be standardized so that the exercise will be the same for all candidates (this includes the situational conditions in addition to the scoring and rating methods). See Thornton and Byham (1982), Feltham (1989) and Woodruffe (1990) for more detail on the design, development and use of AC procedures. The training of assessors will also help to standardize the rating procedures, in addition to ensuring the assessors' competence. Guidance on the training of assessors can be found in Latham and Wexley (1981) and Fay and Latham (1982). If the employing organization's managers are being used as assessors, it is important to ensure that they are at least one or two levels higher in the organization than the level of the job under assessment.

Evaluative standards

As far as criterion-related validity is concerned, assessment centres perform reasonably well. Gaugler et al. (1987) in their meta-analytic review reported a mean *uncorrected* validity coefficient of 0.29. When corrected for statistical artefacts this rose to 0.37. Upon further investigation, it was found that better validities were obtained when more exercises were used, when psychologists rather than managers were the assessors, when peer evaluation was used in the assessment process, when a larger proportion of women were present in the assessee group, and when the proportion of ethnic minority members was small. Surprisingly, the length of assessor training was not found to affect the validity of assessment centres, although it was not possible to assess the quality of the training they received, which arguably may be more important than the length of training. These findings make the point that assessment-centre validity can vary from one setting to another, depending upon the absence or presence of particular features, and that the use of assessment-centre techniques *per se* does not guarantee criterion-related validity.

Some problems have also been found with the construct validity (see Chapter 4) of assessment centres. Beginning with the seminal study of Sackett and Dreher (1982), several other investigators (e.g. Robertson et al., 1987) have shown that correlations *across* dimensions that ostensibly are measuring the same attribute (e.g. leadership skill) are very low, whereas the correlations between different dimensions (e.g. leadership skill and analytical skill) *within* the same exercise are much higher. Further, when factor analyses were conducted on the dimensions under consideration (e.g. leadership, interpersonal relations, planning, problem-solving, etc.) it became clear that the factors represented the different exercises (e.g. in-tray, group discussions, etc.) rather than the dimensions. This is the converse of what would normally be expected if assessment centres had good construct validity. Some evidence exists that an assessor's individual frame of reference when rating candidates might be responsible for these findings. Rather than rating candidates on the dimensions specified by the AC planners, assessors tended to use their own individual categories. This suggests that the use of exercise-specific behavioural checklists and limiting the number of dimensions under assessment might improve construct validity. An additional advantage would be the availability of individual exercise scores that would allow clearer understanding of *what* is being measured, leading to greater understanding of *why* assessment centres predict performance.

Establishing the test–retest reliability of assessment centres can be troublesome because of the difficulties surrounding replication. Ideally, the same applicant cohort would be subjected to two ACs in a short space of time. However, in most instances this would be impractical. Even if it were possible, it would be hard to control various group-dynamic factors simply because applicant–applicant or applicant–assessor relationships may have changed during the first AC, which subsequently may alter both applicant behaviour and assessor judgements during the second AC. Some research has compared the overall ratings of applicants who attended both long and short ACs. They were assessed by different people, on similar exercises that differed in content. The results showed a good correlation between the overall ratings and ratings on specific exercises, suggesting a high test–retest reliability.

In terms of usefulness the evidence from the UK and the USA appears to be fairly conclusive. ACs tend to be rated highly by assessors and successful applicants. From the perspective of the successful applicant, the experience tends to stimulate self-development efforts because it focuses attention on strengths and weaknesses. Similarly, managers serving as assessors tend to learn how to observe systematically and evaluate managerial behaviour, which is normally very difficult in the busy day-to-day mêlée of organizational life. From the organizational perspective some UK research also suggests that assessment centres can play a key role in facilitating organizational change (Guerrier and Riley, 1992). By focusing on organizational change issues within AC exercises, an organization can communicate the message that certain management skills and management styles are important. This may be extremely useful for organizations implementing TQM initiatives. Thus, aside from reasonably accurate personnel selection, all parties involved may derive additional benefits from ACs.

The picture is somewhat different for unsuccessful applicants, who tend to view ACs as being less fair with fewer career benefits. Although it is not known how ACs impact on unsuccessful candidates for entry-level positions, it appears that developmental ACs for existing job holders negatively impact on the unsuccessful applicants' self-esteem, competitiveness and motivation to work; this effect may occur because of the impact that ACs have in terms of highlighting uncertainty over career goals. This suggests that, in order to avoid the loss of staff, the feedback given to unsuccessful applicants should be handled sensitively, perhaps with supportive counselling being made available. With regard to the provision of feedback, Feltham (1989) and others highlight several features of importance. These include the following:

- It should be ensured that the feedback is focused only on the behaviours observed during the AC.
- The feedback should be constructive and of good quality.
- The provision of feedback is a team effort: line managers, HR personnel and at least one of the assessors ought to be involved.
- Feedback should be given face to face, not via written communications.
- The feedback should be linked to a plan of action.
- Feedback should be provided as soon as possible – within a few days if administratively possible.

In terms of unfair discrimination, research suggests ACs also appear to be relatively free from bias in terms of sex and race. One study, however, reported that women applicants for a sales position in a financial services organization obtained higher overall performance ratings than men. This was particularly the case when they were evaluated by an all-male team of assessors, rather than a mixed-sex group. Interestingly, no differences in sales performance were found between successful male and female candidates three years later. This suggests that all-male groups of assessors are more lenient in their ratings of female applicants than of mixed-gender groups of assessors.

Although the effectiveness of assessment centres is being increasingly recognized, relative to other selection procedures they are expensive to prepare and run. However, the available research suggests that the benefits more than outweigh the costs involved. Bedford (1988), for example, showed that in 1985 the annual costs of an AC for selecting seventeen senior police officers to attend the senior command course at the National Police College, Bramhill, was £100,900 or £5,860 per successful candidate. Calculations revealed that, compared to the previous assessment ratings of candidates by their senior officers, the net benefit value of AC procedures was about £800,000. This figure represents a return on investment of about 700 per cent per annum. Similarly, compared to interviews, the Royal

Navy's entry-level assessment centre delivered a net benefit value of £550,000 per annum (Jones, 1988). More recently, an evaluative case study conducted at Ford of Europe was presented, showing how it was possible to reduce the costs of an assessment centre from £788.46 to £187.50 per successful candidate (Payne et al., 1992). It is difficult to calculate a net benefit value for this study because the candidates were seeking sponsorship for an engineering degree course. Any benefits would not be expected to flow until such time as the students passed their degree course and were subsequently employed by the sponsoring organization. Nonetheless, these examples suggest that AC costs can be significantly reduced, while delivering significant financial benefits.

SUMMARY

Task-based methods are among the most valid forms of selection because they focus on what an applicant can do, and because the specific behaviours to be assessed are highly job-related. Additionally, because they are versatile, they can be used for many job classes at different organizational levels. Task-based methods include work-sample tests, trainability tests, job-knowledge tests and assessment centres. Although task-based selection methods are usually more costly to develop and administer, the benefits that may be expected to flow from them can be considerable. They are also relatively free from bias and as such are more easily defendable in unfair discrimination litigation.

8 Selection methods – psychometrics

'Unicare', a recently formed NHS trust, was implementing total quality management (TQM) initiatives, part of which involved a review of staffing. In order to be confident that the delivery of 'patient care' was of the highest quality, the personnel officer was anxious to ensure that, in addition to technical knowledge and skills, every member of staff possessed a high degree of 'service orientation' (SO). This involves treating patients with courtesy, consideration and tact, being receptive to their needs, and being able to communicate in an accurate and pleasant manner.

With the aid of a Chartered Occupational Psychologist, she reviewed all the existing job descriptions with a view to identifying generic categories of duties. Eight were found: five pertaining to technical competency, and three related to service orientation including direct patient services, assistance to other hospital staff, and competent communication. The service-orientation categories and their associated tasks were rated by a group of doctors, senior nurses, administrators and support staff, and the results were used to develop a service-orientation task inventory. The purpose of the inventory was to identify the tasks that were actually critical to the job, in terms of causing patient discomfort or emotional upset. The inventory was subsequently completed by groups of doctors and nursing and support staff from each eight-hour shift; they were asked to evaluate each task in terms of whether or not it was performed on the job and, if so, how frequently, and how important it was for patient care.

On the basis of these evaluations a 92-item personality-based measure and written descriptions of criterion-related behaviour were devised. Trained senior doctors and nurses independently rated the staff under their care on their respective wards. Results indicated high levels of inter-rater reliability, suggesting the measure had practical utility and was consistently measuring the same concepts. Thereafter, to assess its criterion-related validity the measure was administered to one hundred members of staff, whose performance on the job was also rated independently by their supervisors. The correlation between service-orientation scores and job performance was 0.42, indicating that the measure had good criterion-related validity. To ensure that this correlation had not been contaminated by knowledge of the measure's development, it was administered in three other hospitals in the area. Once again, correlations in the region of 0.4 were obtained with supervisory ratings of job performance. Further analyses revealed that it was both sexually and racially neutral and would not lead to unfair discrimination.

The resulting service-orientation index was subsequently administered to all the remaining staff. Those identified as low in service orientation were encouraged to undertake service-orientation training courses. Thereafter, the measure was used in all selection procedures for both trainee and staff positions. Follow-up patient satisfaction surveys at three, six, twelve and twenty-four months indicated that patient care was continually improving, enabling the trust to meet its targets. As a result of these follow-up findings, Unicare made the personality measure available, for a fee, to other hospital trusts, hospitals in the private sector and nursing agencies around the country, enabling them to invest the profits towards desperately needed equipment and keep vital hospital wards open.

The Unicare scenario described above is broadly based on a real-life case study conducted by Hogan et al. (1984) in the USA, and shows that when psychometric measures are developed that focus on specific job-related features, their criterion-related validity can be as good as other selection procedures, although the use of such measures to identify training needs is controversial. Not surprisingly, psychometric measures not focused on job-related features (a common procedure) have been shown to have very little criterion-related validity. The widespread use of psychometric tests for selection purposes in the absence of clear job relevance has fuelled much suspicion, misunderstanding and controversy in industry. For example, the use of clinical personality measures such as the Rorschach 'ink-blot' test, or other tests designed to differentiate between psychotics, psychopaths, etc., in the workplace, is a case in point. Clearly, these types of test are not very useful for predicting work behaviour, unless of course a psychopath is required!

This uncontrolled use of psychometric tests has recently led the British Psychological Society (BPS) to require occupational test users to be properly trained and certificated. In addition to the BPS (Bartram and Lindley, 1994), many reputable test suppliers provide the necessary training courses to enable lay people to conduct psychometric testing to BPS standards. Any organization considering the use of psychometric measures for selection purposes must ensure that properly trained personnel are available.

PSYCHOLOGICAL TESTING

Two major types of psychological tests are used by personnel selection practitioners: tests of cognitive ability and personality measures. Broadly speaking, cognitive tests provide assessments of the kind of intellectual abilities mentioned in Chapter 2 when individual differences in human intellectual abilities were discussed. Many commercial cognitive tests are available for assessing general intelligence g and its various sub-components such as spatial ability, numerical ability and verbal ability. Personality measures, on the other hand, are more concerned with people's disposition to behave in certain ways in certain situations.

Cognitive testing

Of all of the available personnel selection methods, the evidence concerning cognitive tests is certainly the most extensive and conclusive. Very many studies of the criterion-related validity of cognitive tests have been carried out in the UK, the USA, and several other countries involving hundreds of thousands of people. Until the late 1970s psychologists felt that although cognitive tests had value in some situations there was no clear consensus that they could be used to good effect in all settings. Most believed that for a cognitive test or any other selection procedure to be useful, it was necessary to conduct an organization specific criterion-related validation study. This view was based on the fact that the size of the validity coefficients obtained for cognitive tests differed across many studies, often by some large margin. At that time, many investigators failed to realize that small sample sizes, which researchers tended to use, caused much of the variation in the study results. During the late 1970s and early 1980s two American researchers (Jack Hunter and Frank Schmidt) transformed psychologists' views of the evidence concerning the validity of most selection methods and cognitive tests in particular. In a series of very influential articles Schmidt and Hunter (see Murphy, 1988 for a review) showed that when adjustments were made for various factors, such as sample size and restrictions in the range of scores available, the studies of cognitive-ability tests gave remarkably consistent results. These results showed, quite clearly, that cognitive tests were valid in a wide range of settings. In other words, such tests could be used to predict people's performance in most jobs.

For obvious reasons this finding has major implications for personnel selection practice. It implies that a test of general mental ability (g) should be considered for inclusion in any selection procedure. To the non-psychologist the evidence for the criterion-related validity of g is a little tricky to interpret. This is because most of the key analyses make use of an advanced statistical technique (meta-analysis, Hunter and Schmidt, 1990), the results of which are not reported in a consistent way. For example, although investigators in all meta-analytic studies make some adjustments to the raw data, some make several 'corrections' to the coefficient whereas others do not. Because of this it is important to be clear about the adjustments that have been made to reported coefficients, before deciding how to interpret them. Often the (uncorrected) coefficients obtained for tests of g are no larger than those for other well regarded selection procedures. Nonetheless, the striking thing about the results for g is that there is relatively little variation from one setting to another and, as suggested above, tests of general mental ability are worth considering in almost every setting. Such tests are quick and simple to administer and, as long as there is a trained person available, their interpretation is fairly straightforward. Sometimes there are perfectly good reasons for discounting the use of a test of g. One example of a setting where such a test would be of limited value is when the candidates are all likely to have similar levels of ability (e.g. when graduates are being selected).

Another situation where the case for using a test of general mental ability needs to be evaluated more carefully is when there is a possibility of bias against members of ethnic or other specific subgroups of the population. Consistent research results have shown that people from certain ethnic groups (e.g. black Americans) have a tendency to score less well on tests of cognitive ability. The same is also true of people from certain socio-economic groups. Interestingly, it is possible to produce tests that give discrepancies in either direction: for example, the Black Intelligence Test of Cultural Homogeneity (BITCH) gives higher scores for black Americans. Obviously if cognitive tests form part of a selection procedure, the people who attain lower scores on them will come out less well in the overall process and correspondingly will be less likely to be selected. This should be a source of serious concern for selection decision-makers, for social, ethical and technical reasons. There is no simple solution to the problem since no one has yet been successful in devising an intelligence test that does not produce discrepancies in scores between subgroups. These problems with cognitive tests have led some people to be very negative about their use in personnel selection. Others argue that since the tests are good, generalized predictors of job success it is foolish to discontinue their use.

It is important to distinguish between the criterion-related validity of a test and the potential negative impact that it may have on some specific subgroup. Most psychologists accept that a test is fair to different subgroups if it does not make more errors of prediction for one group than any other (Cleary, 1968). In other words, a test is fair if it predicts the work performance of all groups equally well. This seems a perfectly sensible way of looking at the fairness of tests. The research evidence available to date shows quite clearly that cognitive tests do not give significantly more errors of prediction for one group than another (see Schmitt and Noe, 1986). Unfortunately, ensuring that a test is fair does not ensure that some groups will not produce lower performance. For instance, a test of spatial ability would probably produce slightly lower scores for female candidates whereas a test of verbal ability would almost certainly favour females. Either test could be a perfectly good predictor of performance at some tasks for both groups. Choosing smaller numbers of candidates from some subgroups is often socially unacceptable and the role that tests of cognitive ability should play, in any particular personnel selection system, needs to be evaluated in each separate set of circumstances. Despite the difficulties involved, there are many situations where it is beneficial for both candidates and organizations to use cognitive tests. In this regard, there is a regularly updated comprehensive review of the majority of cognitive tests that are currently available in the UK (Bartram et al., 1990).

Personality measures

Self-report personality inventories provide a convenient way of gaining a picture of candidates' disposition. The major dimensions of personality were outlined in Chapter 2. For the purposes of personnel selection the crucial question concerning personality tests is: 'Do they provide information that may be used to derive more accurate predictions of people's subsequent work behaviour?' Although firm evidence has become available only relatively recently, the answer to this question seems to be 'yes'. Perhaps this does not seem surprising. Dispositional factors such as emotional stability and extroversion play a considerable role in our everyday life and there seems no reason to expect that they will not have some effect on work performance.

During the 1980s meta-analytic techniques were used to examine the validity of personality measures in much the same way that the criterion-related validity of mental ability testing was explored. The results of the first studies were much less positive than those obtained for mental ability testing (see Schmitt et al., 1984). Subsequent studies (see Robertson, 1993, 1994 for a review) have produced more positive findings but have also provided some important messages about how personality instruments need to be much more carefully designed than was at first thought. In essence these have demonstrated the need for the personality constructs under investigation to be linked to specific job competencies, that in themselves have been linked to job performance (see Figure 8.1). For example, Conscientiousness (personality trait) is related to a tendency to set goals (job competency) which is linked with greater productivity (job performance) in jobs where the incumbent has discretion about his or her activities.

The most important evidence concerning personality measures comes from a series of meta-analytic studies reported in the early 1990s (Tett et al., 1991; Barrick and Mount, 1991; Robertson and Kinder, 1993). The important finding of these studies was that, when used in a *focused way*, personality measures could produce validity coefficients of worthwhile magnitude, as illustrated in the Unicare example.

In an important methodological development Tett et al. (1991) showed that, when studies used a priori hypotheses and job analyses to identify personality characteristics, validity coefficients were much better than when these steps were not taken. Their study made use of the 'Big Five' framework and found the best overall validity for Agreeableness (0.22). This was not directly in line with the results of Barrick and Mount who found little evidence of criterion-related validity for Agreeableness but found good results for Conscientiousness and Openness to Experience. Robertson and Kinder (1993) used predetermined hypotheses to investigate the criterion-related validity of various personality constructs drawn from the Occupational Personality Questionnaire, a test designed specifically for use in industrial settings (see Chapter 2). They found validities that varied from 0.09 to over 0.30 for characteristics such as Adaptability (0.09), Resilience (0.20) and Analysis (0.32).

There is certainly not yet enough conclusive evidence to draw firm conclusions about the validity of specific personality constructs for particular occupational areas, as the different results from the different investigations mentioned above make clear. There is, however, sufficient evidence to suggest that the thoughtful and controlled use of personality tests has a place in personnel selection. For example, researchers have shown that Openness to Experience (i.e. intelligence, curiosity and broad-mindedness) and Extroversion (i.e. talkative, active, assertive) are associated with training success across many diverse occupations. Similarly, salespeople high in Conscientiousness (i.e. hardworking, persistent, achievement-oriented) are more likely to set goals, which in turn is associated with

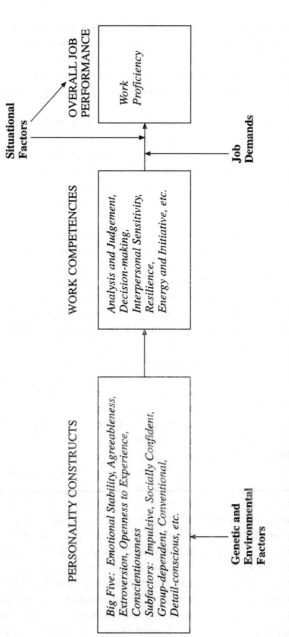

Figure 8.1 Personality–competency–performance links

greater sales volume and higher supervisory ratings of job perform-ance. Moreover, Conscientiousness and Extroversion are both strongly linked with managerial performance, particularly when the job holder has a large degree of autonomy. Conversely, those high in Agreeableness (i.e. courteous, forgiving, trusting) perform less well with high degrees of autonomy, demonstrating how situational demands and dispositional factors combine to influence performance. As a whole these studies have established that specific personality features are related to specific aspects of job performance, manifestly demonstrating the importance of avoiding the 'blunderbuss' approach to personality testing.

This view is reflected in strongly expressed critical comments made by some psychologists about the general use of personality measures in personnel selection. Some of the critical comments raised concern the need for investigators to take care in the methodology used when exploring the validity of personality meas-ures. These comments are a useful antidote to the tendency that some people have of making indiscriminate use of personality measures, on the assumption that some useful information about candidates will be bound to be revealed. General personality measures may well produce some important information about candidates; however, without clear ideas about what to look for, based on a detailed job analysis and other sources, the selector may well not be able to separate the signal from the noise.

One final finding from the research evidence is worth noting. In their study Robertson and Kinder (1993) addressed the question of whether or not personality tests provided additional useful informa-tion about candidates' work behaviour. Obviously, if the information from personality measures can be obtained by other, simpler means, then there is no need to go to the time and trouble of using personality tests in the selection process. The specific issue that Robertson and Kinder looked at was whether or not personality tests added anything useful to the criterion-related validity obtained from cognitive tests alone. The answer was conclusive and showed that the information of relevance to candidates' work behaviour carried by personality measures did not duplicate that provided by cognitive tests.

Specific personality tests

Although many personality tests are available, relatively few have been specifically developed for use in industrial settings. One of the most frequently used in personnel selection is the 16PF which was developed in the USA and has been widely researched and validated. There are four parallel forms of the 16PF: Forms A and B are long versions, each asking 187 questions, while Forms C and D are short parallel forms each consisting of 105 questions. However, these short versions were developed for other purposes and should not be used in personnel selection. It is possible with the A and B forms to use 'specification equations' to calculate scores on other factors such as leadership potential, ability to integrate into a new job, creativity, etc. The popularity of the 16PF is probably related to the fact that the handbook gives specification equations for almost a hundred different occupations.

A British personality measure, specifically designed for the workplace, is the Occupational Personality Questionnaire (OPQ), developed by Saville and Holdsworth Ltd in 1985. It is not a single questionnaire, but a series of nine interlocking questionnaires that vary in length and format, with the user choosing the level of detail required for the job in question. The longest versions consist of thirty concepts. The shorter versions measure a number of factors derived from the thirty concepts. Three different rating formats are also used, incorporating yes/no responses, rating scales and forced-choice questions. It is recommended that two pairs of rating format be used. However, administrators must be trained, as interpretation can take an experienced user between one and two hours.

Many other personality measures are available in the commercial arena, some more useful than others. The persuasiveness of the test salesperson may determine the test an organization might use, rather than its technical properties. It would appear that hard-nosed managers are often a soft touch when it comes to personality measures. Research specifically conducted on this issue is very illuminating. A group of personnel managers attending a conference were asked to complete a published personality test. Unbeknown to them, instead of giving them their actual scores, they were all given an identical series of personality statements derived from astrology books. An example of one of the statements is 'At times you are extroverted, affable and sociable, while at other times you are introverted, wary and reserved'. Each manager was then asked to rate the accuracy of these statements, with 80 per cent of them indicating that their personal profile was either very good or amazingly accurate. This research illustrates the point that technical adequacy must reign supreme, even though making choice. tests can seem a nightmare. A comprehensive revi. tests for use in occupational testing is available (Bartram, 1995) in addition to information conce petencies required for users of these tests (British Society, 1994).

Users ought to be guided by the personality instrument's relevance to the personnel specifications derived from job analyses in addition to its psychometric properties, particularly in terms of reliability and validity. Once these factors have been determined, Smith and Robertson (1993) suggest that it may be useful to focus on other considerations such as:

- Costs: training of test administrators, test booklets and answer sheets; manuals and scoring keys, annual licence fees.
- Time: delivery, which may take several months; the amount of time required to administer the test; time required for scoring; costs of scoring by test developer/supplier.
- Adequacy of Manual, which might include:
  (a) ease of understanding;
  (b) clear statement of purpose of test;
  (c) clear instructions for test administration;
  (d) clear instructions for scoring of test;
  (e) validity and reliability studies needed for correct interpretation of scores;
  (f) norms for relevant occupational groups.

In addition, focusing on information about how the test was designed and constructed, and any comments made by reviewers, would be useful.

Faking

One area of potential concern to selectors is the degree to which responses to personality tests might be faked. Faking is usually termed 'social desirability' and is thought to comprise two elements: self-deception and impression management (Paulhaus, 1989). Self-deception refers to applicants' being overly optimistic in their perceptions of positive personality features while simultaneously trying to play down their perceived negative aspects. Impression management is more concerned with applicants trying to appear 'nice' because they fear social disapproval. In combination, these two aspects may lead people to try and put up a 'good front' when completing self-report measures.

Although a large stream of research evidence exists to show that many personality tests are fakeable, much of this research has been conducted with undergraduate students who have been directed to falsify their responses. Research conducted with real job applicants suggests that the vast majority do not fake their responses. For example, Hough et al. (1990), in a criterion-related validity study, compared the responses of 245 'fakers' (existing job holders) with 125 job applicants. The fakers successfully distorted their self-descriptions when instructed to do so, whereas the applicants' responses did not reflect any evidence of distortion. Significantly, regardless of faking, the criterion-related validities of the various personality constructs remained stable. Indeed, the notion that social-desirability responding has very little effect on most organizational behaviour research has received considerable support in a recent meta-analytic study for a wide range of organizational variables (Moorman and Podsakoff, 1992).

Nonetheless, for those selectors who consider faking to be a real problem, possible defences include:

- warning people about the possible consequences of faking (e.g. not hiring them);
- developing 'lie detection' scales (this is usually best left to experts such as Chartered Occupational Psychologists);
- using additional, or other, information such as 'integrity tests' (see later in this chapter) to make decisions about those identified as faking.

BIODATA

The use of biographical data as a selection procedure is an interesting and sometimes controversial topic, even though meta-analytic studies have revealed that 'biodata' provide reasonably good criterion-related validity (Hunter and Hunter, 1984). Like several of the other personnel selection methods discussed in this book, biodata have several unique features that distinguish them from other approaches. The most striking of these is that *some* biodata instruments (actuarial) are *not* linked to the tasks involved in a job. Instead, they involve reliance on statistical links between particular life events or candidate characteristics and future performance, rather than any psychological links between predictor and criterion. The available evidence suggests that these instruments can predict various important aspects of job performance.

Biographical data are collected in two main ways: application forms and biographical questionnaires. The essential difference between the two methods resides in the amount and types of information collected. Application forms request limited amounts of information such as age, marital status and previous employment history. Biographical questionnaires provide detailed life-history information. They may also tap into other psychological constructs such as a person's locus of control, assertiveness and independence, and thus, to some extent, emulate personality tests. This has led to the blurring of distinctions between biographical questionnaires and personality inventories. Nonetheless, two key features distinguish biographical measures from personality measures: first, unlike personality measures, most biographical questionnaires are job-specific, and, second, the scoring procedures are quite different. Most biographical items are quite clear about the information required and allow specific answers that, in theory, could be answered by someone who knows the respondent well (e.g. his or her mother). Even when particular psychological constructs are being investigated, multiple-choice answers are provided which specify the information required. Personality inventories, on the other hand, are phrased in ways that elicit rapid responses, typically with some form of rating scale. Further, the scoring procedures of personality tests remain the same over extended periods of time. The scoring procedure for biographical questionnaires need to be updated every three to five years, particularly when changes occur in the job, the criterion or the original applicant group.

Competing alternatives

The fundamentals of the biodata approach involve identifying correlations between items of biographical information (e.g. education, membership of societies, employment history, etc.) and criterion measures (e.g. work performance, absenteeism). Two alternative approaches to developing biodata items exist. The first is termed the *empirical* approach whereby statistical profiles of various demographic variables (e.g. age, sex, marital status, number of dependents, etc.) have been shown to be related to turnover, absenteeism, accident rates, or success in the job.

Most of the problems associated with the use of biodata arise from the uncritical use of these empirically derived items. For example, in one often-quoted use of a biodata questionnaire, one of the most predictive items concerned the vacation habits of the candidate. The large weighting assigned to this item was based on a purely statistical link between the item and candidates' job performance. In fact, the item was specifically about whether candidates took holidays in Spain (with the answer 'yes' being weighted negatively)! A logical, or job-related, basis for this item is difficult to see. In other words, it appears not to matter *why* these profiles are predictive, only that they *are*. This is a poor basis for making selection decisions and may lead to unintentional discrimination against certain people or groups.

With these problems in mind, the *rational* approach to the development of biodata, which involves clear hypotheses about specific job-relevant constructs, has been utilized. This approach is in line with attempts by some authors to develop a theoretical rationale for the predictive validity of biodata. Owens and colleagues (e.g. Neiner and Owens, 1982), on the basis that past behaviour predicts future behaviour, proposed two broad classes of biodata: environmental inputs and prior experiences. They suggest that people with similar patterns of environmental inputs and prior experiences can be classified into subgroups, as they are likely to behave in similar ways. The predictive element of this model comes from the fact that people from one subgroup will behave differently from people in other subgroups, and therefore it is simply a matter of matching the attributes of each subgroup to the required job characteristics.

Others, however, suggest that the Owens model concentrates too much on the characteristics of individuals and not enough on situational features. In an attempt to balance individual and situational factors, Drakeley (1989) proposed a triple biodata classification system: situational factors, termed 'background' data; motivational factors related to an individual's needs and expectations, termed 'commitment' biodata; and, previous experiences, termed 'achievement' biodata. In an attempt to predict the training success and turnover of trainee Royal Navy officers, Drakeley et al. (1988) compared the efficacy of the triple biodata model with an overall assessment rating (OAR) and a composite test score, derived from four psychometric tests of intellectual aptitude. Results showed that the predictive validity of the biodata for professional examination success was pretty much the same as the OAR and composite test scores. For the prediction of leadership scores, biodata was better than the composite score, but worse than the OAR. However, the biodata did predict withdrawal from training (turnover), which the other methods failed to do.

Thus some empirical evidence supports the triple biodata model, although further research is still required. More recent developments have linked human developmental theories to biodata (e.g. Mumford et al. 1991), with the result that these biodata inventories include more 'soft' subjective items than previously had been the case, indicating a move towards more personality-type measures. Indeed, Stokes and Reddy (1992) explored the use of biodata items as measures of psychological, as opposed to statistical, constructs and identified some common ground between the use of biodata and personality assessment. Overall, the rational approach is clearly much more appealing from the explanatory point of view, although evidence to date suggests that it has slightly poorer validity than the empirical approach. Gains in fairness and understanding may, however, outweigh this loss of validity.

Developing biodata inventories

Initially, job analyses are conducted with existing job holders to identify important job-related behaviours/attributes. These are then developed into performance-based biodata items. If, for example, 'leadership potential' were deemed to be an important feature of a job, the corresponding biodata item(s) might be evidence of accepting (or not accepting) prior responsibility (e.g. captain of a sports team, school prefect, editor of a magazine, etc.). Similarly, the ability to work in a team may be tapped by specific biodata items asking about membership of clubs and societies. At the same time, the appropriate criterion measures, identified via the job analyses, are chosen or developed.

Once the biodata items and the criterion measures have been developed, two decisions have to be made. One concerns the degree of correspondence between them, and the other concerns the scoring procedures to be used. Correlations between the biodata items and criterion measures are established empirically by conducting a predictive or (more often) concurrent validation study (see Chapter 4). Biodata items that predict the criterion are then combined into a questionnaire which may be administered to applicants. Once these results have been checked by cross-validation on a different sample, information from the validation stage can be used to provide a scoring procedure.

The scoring of biodata items is normally done by using some form of weighting system. These may be determined by expert judgements, although this method is not particularly effective as it relies on intuitive judgements concerning the likely relationships between the items and the criterion. Objective scoring can be determined in one of two ways: first, individual items are weighted by their ability to predict performance, most commonly with the use of the per cent method (see Drakeley, 1989); second, factor analysis is used to identify meaningful clusters of items (e.g. all the items pertaining to past achievements), which are then weighted as composite scores.

Evaluative standards

In terms of their criterion-related validity, recent meta-analytic reviews suggest that biodata compare well with cognitive ability tests in predicting training success (0.50) and entry-level job performance (0.37), and are superior to other methods for predicting turnover (0.24). Nonetheless, biodata inventories have to be re-visited every three to five years to ensure their accuracy. The main disadvantage of biodata inventories resides in the fact that they are specific to a particular job class (e.g. clerical), and cannot, in the normal course of events, be used for other job classes. This means that a separate biodata inventory has to be developed for each type of job class, which can be expensive.

Most considerations of bias induced by biodata have been conducted on American populations. Reilly and Chao (1982), in their review, investigated racial and gender biases in relation to biodata, and concluded that little bias was found for race, but strong evidence was found for bias effects against women. Similarly, others have consistently found that females are given lower evaluations than men, particularly when the jobs in question are thought to be masculine in nature. Other evidence also suggests strong bias against older workers. Conversely, in a UK military setting no bias has been found for socioeconomic or educational variables. Overall, this evidence suggests that the use of biodata is potentially open to litigation on the grounds of fairness, unless care is taken, perhaps by the use of rational procedures for item development or by developing separate instruments for males and females, and for young and older workers.

Biodata inventories are very useful and cost-effective tools when used in the pre-selection screening process, particularly for organizations that routinely select from a large pool of applicants. Scoring is reduced to a clerical activity and can be done by anyone by simply calculating a total score. Alternatively, as is already the case in many UK companies, the scores can be processed by desk-top computers. However, the costs of constructing a biodata inventory can be exorbitant if used for small numbers of applicants. Cost–benefit analyses (see Chapter 5) can help to determine the viability of biodata instruments for any particular organization.

Recent studies have examined the faking of biodata inventories. The results indicated that they can be faked, but little faking occurred in practice. Most of the faked items were more subjective than historical, objective items. For example, Stokes et al. (1993), in a study conducted with 2,262 incumbent sales representatives and 2,726 applicants for sales positions, found that faking was minimal for item categories such as previous work experience and economic motivation, but was more prevalent in categories such as work style, work preferences and self-evaluations of prior sales success. Other research shows that faking is minimized when applicants are warned against it and when the items are transparent and objective.

INTEGRITY TESTING

For many jobs it is essential that employees are honest, particularly those involved in the handling of money, or other goods that can easily be converted into money. Under these circumstances, it is natural for organizations to try to find valid and reliable methods for detecting dishonest applicants, prior to employment.

One approach to detecting dishonest applicants is the use of the 'lie detector' or 'polygraph'. Lie detectors work by detecting changes in electrical resistance on the skin (conductance) or changes in breathing rates (respiration) that are a result of fear or anxiety. Originally, they were designed to detect whether or not someone was lying about a specific event (e.g. a crime). As a pre-employment screening test they are used in a more generalized way, with no specific event being investigated. When used in this way, the applicant's responses to loaded questions (e.g. 'Have you ever stolen from your previous employer?') are compared to his or her responses to neutral questions (e.g. 'Do you always eat eggs for breakfast?').

The problem with the lie detector is that honest people who are nervous about the test may appear to be dishonest. Applicants who are dishonest may not be detected if they remain calm and do not respond physiologically. Because of this fundamental flaw, nineteen states in the USA have 'outlawed' the use of polygraphs for selection purposes. Despite their flawed nature, the British government attempted to introduce polygraphs to 'vet' employees involved in intelligence and security in 1983. This was resisted by the trade unions, until the attempt was abandoned. Although the use of polygraphs is legal in the UK, sufficient published evidence is available for the British Psychological Society to disapprove of its use as an honesty test for selection purposes.

A better method for ascertaining an applicant's integrity is provided by 'paper-and-pencil' questionnaires. These tests tend to be of two varieties: overt and personality-based. Overt tests openly focus on the applicants' previous behaviour (e.g. 'Have you ever been convicted for theft?') or attitudes towards crime (e.g. 'Should this company fire employees caught stealing?'). In contrast, personality-based tests have a much broader focus in that they attempt to measure counter-productive work behaviours such as an applicant's propensity to take extended work breaks, abuse of sick-leave systems, disciplinary problems, drug abuse and violence. In essence these measures focus on an applicant's responsibility, reliability and conscientiousness. The distinctions between the two types of integrity tests were supported in a factor-analytic study of integrity tests conducted by Woolley and Hakstian (1992). Detailed descriptions of many integrity tests can be found in *The Tenth Mental Measurements Yearbook* (Conoley and Kramer, 1989).

Although a fairly recent development, the published research indicates that both types of questionnaires successfully discriminate between honest and dishonest applicants. Typically, overt tests and personality-based tests are validated against different criteria. Most overt tests are compared with the results of polygraph tests and indices of theft such as self-report measures of illegal activity. Personality-based tests are typically compared with supervisory ratings of job performance or objective data held in personnel files such as the number of absences. A recent study compared the utility of a personality test, a personality-based integrity test and biodata inventory to discriminate white-collar 'criminals' from other white collar employees. The personality-based integrity test was best and revealed that offenders scored low on social conscientiousness and tended to be irresponsible and unreliable with a disregard for rules and social norms.

Evaluative standards

In terms of criterion-related validity for predicting overall job performance, meta-analyses indicate the mean validity coefficient for personality-based honesty tests is 0.35 as compared with 0.33 for overt tests (Ones et al., 1993). Moreover, both types of test predicted applicants' counter-productive behaviours better than those for existing job holders. For personality tests this was 0.29 compared to 0.26, whereas for overt tests this difference was somewhat larger (0.39 vs 0.9). This evidence suggests that these tests do have criterion-related validity and may be of some use to organizations.

In terms of reliability, the evidence suggests that the average internal consistency for overt tests (0.83) is slightly higher than for personality-based tests (0.72), which perhaps is not surprising. Nonetheless, these data suggest that these tests are fairly reliable. In a series of research studies conducted during the late 1980s the test scores of ethnic minorities did not differ from any other, suggesting that bias is not systematically introduced. However, no research appears to have been conducted for bias on the grounds of gender. Ones et al. also suggest that if employers seeking to maximize productivity used a composite measure of integrity and ability, cost-benefit ratios could be improved by as much as 58 per cent, in comparison with selecting for ability alone. This is in addition to the benefits expected to flow from the reduction of counter-productive behaviours.

SUMMARY

The many forms of psychometric measures that are focused on job-related features have been shown to be valid predictors of work behaviour and job performance. Conversely, those not related to job-related features are not particularly useful. Many reviews have indicated that cognitive tests which measure general mental ability (g) are valid in the majority of work settings. The focused use of personality tests also has much to commend their use in many work-settings, particularly as they add value beyond that carried by cognitive tests. However, selectors need to exercise considerable caution when choosing personality tests. Biodata inventories also have much to offer in predicting job performance, and are very useful for screening out unsuitable applicants prior to undertaking in-depth selection procedures. Similarly, integrity testing offers much in the way of screening out dishonest applicants. Decisions about which form of psychometric testing is used should be guided by technical adequacy and the test's relevance to the personnel specifications derived from job analyses, rather than the persuasiveness of salespeople.

9 Selection methods – alternatives?

'Rainbow', a large international blue-chip company, had been so successful that its cash surplus was approaching £3 billion. The board decided to treat its treasury department as a separate profit centre and was looking for a new fund manager to manage its investment portfolio. Because this was a new strategy the board did not want to rattle its shareholders and decided that, rather than advertising the post, they would appoint an executive search company to find the right person. Keyplayers was chosen because the chief executive's son had been headhunted by them for an executive position on the board of a recently privatized utility company.

Keyplayers began its research into possible candidates by identifying approximately two hundred high-profile individuals from trade journals, directories, professional lists, national newspapers and management magazines. Using their network of 'personal' contacts, the candidates were discreetly checked out without their knowledge. This was to see if they were responsible for good or poor company results and what their general reputations were with their peers. The field was gradually narrowed down to fifteen people identified as rising stars. On the basis of personal information that Keyplayers had gleaned from various sources, they obtained copies of each potential candidate's birth certificate from St Catherine's

House in London. They gave these to an eminent astrologer who often provided forecasts about candidates to the company. With knowledge of the exact time and place of birth of each candidate, a personal astrological chart was constructed for each. Six of the candidates had been born when Mars had just reached its highest point in the sky. The astrologer informed Keyplayers that this was significant, as this planetary position was related to the fortunes of many very eminent people.

These six potential candidates were subsequently invited to lunch at an exclusive club. Lunch was for an informal chat where impressions could be formed and where the job could be 'sold' to them. Before leaving the club, the four who expressed an interest were asked to write down the names of three referees, a little bit about themselves in terms of how good they thought they were in relation to their peers, and their perceived career progression over the next ten years. Keyplayers forwarded these scripts to an eminent graphologist who was asked to assess each candidate's personality from the handwriting samples. When these 'personality profiles' were returned, Keyplayers matched those provided by the graphologist with those of the astrologer. Although none of the profiles matched, one set of profiles was similar in so far as both had identified the candidate as outgoing and highly motivated. Because this accorded with their own impressions of the person, Keyplayers contacted the three referees provided by their preferred candidate. Although they were informed that the candidate had already been in touch with each referee in advance to provide the necessary background, Keyplayers accepted the positive ratings from each. Keyplayers went back to Rainbow and informed them that, after extensive enquiries and 'personality profiling', they had found the ideal fund manager, who would fit in well in the organization. This resulted in one candidate being offered and accepting a five-year rolling contract as fund manager at £100,000 per annum, with considerable benefits such as share options, health care, etc. Eighteen months later, the board of Rainbow wanted to increase its dividend to shareholders substantially, but discovered to its horror that the company had lost about £500 million due to a bond-market crash. This was because the new fund manager had switched funds from low-risk deposit accounts and invested heavily in high-yield mortgage-backed and derivative-related bonds and 'swaps' because of falling interest rates. At the annual general meeting the shareholders were furious that they had not been informed of the new strategy of treating the treasury department as an investment centre. After just surviving a vote of no-confidence, the CEO dismissed the new fund manager. Ironically, because of his five-year rolling contract, which did not have a performance-related clause, he went with a 'golden handshake' of £400,000.

As the Rainbow example illustrates, some of the more colourful selection methods have little validity and can cost employing companies vast sums of money. In the words of one psychologist who has investigated such methods, 'You might as well take a stack of applications and throw them out of the window, then choose those that land face up' (McLeod, 1994). As the authors have tried to make clear throughout this book, a thorough job analysis and the use of reliable and valid selection methods is the cornerstone of good selection. The methods described in this chapter differ from those in previous chapters and are somewhat controversial because in the main they are not based on job analyses. In addition, they are not in common usage, their validity is suspect, or they discriminate unfairly between applicants.

PEER ASSESSMENT

A vast body of research stretching back to the 1920s has found that peer assessments are a good way of predicting those who will succeed *within* an organization. In terms of selecting external applicants, however, they are of little use, mainly because of the impracticality of obtaining the assessments from identifiable groups of peers. Nonetheless, unbeknown to potential candidates, discreet verbal peer assessments are commonly sought by executive search agencies for senior-management positions, as the Rainbow example illustrates. In the main, however, peer assessments are used for identifying or confirming an individual's potential for promotion within an organization.

Typically, a group of colleagues who are of equal status make the assessment, as they have the opportunity to observe each other's work behaviour in various situations on a daily basis. This peer group make judgements about, or choices between, one another according to specific criteria, but are not allowed to nominate themselves. Three methods of peer assessment can be found in the literature: peer nominations, whereby each member of the group nominates and ranks individuals as being good or poor; peer ranking, where each member rank orders all the other group members; and peer ratings, where each member rates all the other members on some scale. Love (1981) found that the reliability and predictive validity of nominations and ranking were better than those of ratings. In terms of validity, impressive results have consistently been reported across a wide variety of settings and with different criteria. Dobson (1989) reported that the average sample-weighted coefficient is 0.5 for peer nominations, 0.43 for peer rankings and 0.39 for peer ratings. Peer assessments also appear to show better agreement with supervisory ratings than self-assessments. Harris and Schaubroeck (1988), for example, obtained correlations of 0.48 when corrected for sampling error, and 0.62 when corrected for other artefacts. These correlations indicate that peers are far less lenient in their assessments than would be expected.

Personnel managers often dismiss the use of peer assessments, due to beliefs that they will only provide information about an individual's popularity, despite evidence that friendship does not affect the performance ratings of peers. More often than not, however, it is the peer group themselves who adversely react to these assessments, as they are not so keen on evaluating each other. It has been suggested that this is because peer assessments can easily infringe on other areas that will raise havoc with the group or cause resistance to making the assessments. However, when used for career counselling the peer assessments are seen as useful feedback, which suggests that the purpose of the assessments will determine people's reactions to their use.

SELF-ASSESSMENT

Measures of personality and the like depend on self-reports provided by a respondent. Recent innovations have extended self-reports to provide measures of an individual's abilities, skills, knowledge and performance. Self-assessment is essentially the same as any other self-report, except that applicants are asked to make direct estimates of their own abilities or competencies. As illustrated in the Rainbow example, these estimates are usually based on comparisons with others (e.g. 'How good a programmer are you, compared to other programmers you know: average, below average or above average?'). In practical terms these assessments are cheap and easy to obtain and are unlikely to be challenged by applicants as unfair. But how useful are they?

Some research conducted during the late 1970s and early 1980s indicates that applicants are fairly good at judging their own abilities. Others have found this to be the case only when assessments were for straightforward, well-understood tasks. For more complex tasks very little support was found for their use. These studies also find that applicants tend to overestimate their abilities. In one study, 40 per cent of applicants placed themselves in the top 10 per cent! Only a small percentage placed themselves below average. In another study, typists were found to overestimate their typing speed by about 30 per cent. These studies suggest that leniency effects are common in self-assessment, a viewpoint confirmed by more recent research. The introduction of leniency effects during self-assessments is probably related to the fact that people try to maintain a positive self-image of themselves. Nonetheless, leniency may explain why the validity of self-assessment is poor. Reilly and Chao (1982), for example, reviewed ten studies of self-assessment directly relevant to the selection context and obtained a validity coefficient of 0.15. Another review of fifty-five studies on self-assessments of ability, skill and knowledge, estimated the validity coefficient at about 0.29. Because few of these were conducted in selection situations, this may be an overestimate of the practical validity of self-assessment. Researchers exploring the theoretical reasons for discrepancies between self- and supervisory ratings argue that future-oriented self-assessments be used for developmental purposes only.

Taken as a whole this body of evidence suggests that, currently, self-assessments have little to offer in the selection process. This may change in the near future, as other research on self-assessment utilizes the construct of 'self-efficacy', derived from Bandura's (1977, 1986) social learning theory. Self-efficacy is defined as one's judgement of 'how well one can execute courses of action required to deal with prospective situations'. Thus self-efficacy is concerned with estimates of a person's capacity to perform at a certain level, while taking into account all relevant factors such as ability, effort, adaptability, attributions and situational factors. Broadly speaking, self-efficacy is measured by asking applicants to rate their confidence in reaching a number of performance levels within a given task (see Moe and Zeiss, 1982 for more details). Researchers have shown that self-efficacy scores are good predictors of work performance. For example, self-efficacy is positively related to work attendance and sales performance. Interestingly, one group of researchers found that self-efficacy predicted the performance of personnel selectors in job interviews. Similarly, Robertson and Sadri (1993, see below) have devised a measure of managerial self-efficacy and found that this correlated with independent supervisory ratings of performance.

Items from a managerial self-efficacy scale
When making your best effort would you be able to:

- Analyse statistical reports or other statistical data?
- Set priorities for work assigned to individuals?
- Discuss work problems with subordinates?
- Negotiate with others in order to reach an agreement or solution?
- Chair or lead a meeting?
- Develop, approve or negotiate performance objectives for individuals?

Each item is rated on an anchored scale from 0 (a lot worse than my peers) to 100 (completely better than my peers).

Moreover, Sadri and Robertson (1993), in a study that drew together all the relevant previous work, showed that self-efficacy correlated with work-related behaviour across a wide range of activities and occupational areas. This evidence suggests that in the not too distant future self-efficacy measures may prove to be a valid and reliable method for developing self-assessment indicators.

GRAPHOLOGY

Graphology – the study of handwriting – is based on the notion that handwriting reveals something about a person's personality, from which inferences about that person's behaviour can be made. Supporters of graphology claim that it offers a personality profile as accurate as any other method at a fraction of the cost. For example, claims are made that untidy handwriting reveals an untidy person or that bold handwriting reveals an aggressive, assertive personality. These claims are made on the assumption that the muscles which control writing reflect unconscious impulses in the brain.

In the context of selection, if the inferences are accurate, they may be of some value in the decision-making process. Certainly, continental Europeans think so, particularly the French, as 77 per cent of smaller French companies use graphology to select their managers (Smith and Abrahamsen, 1992). This finding is probably related to the fact that half of all French executive search companies use graphology. The use of graphology is less common in the UK. Fewer than 3 per cent of UK 'headhunters' admit to using graphology. Two UK companies known to use graphology for selection are the merchant bankers SG Warburg, who appear to be somewhat bashful about admitting its use, and the conglomerate Heron International, which has used it as part of the managerial selection procedure since 1986. The head of the International Grapho-analysis Society believes 3 per cent of UK companies, many in the *Times* Top 1000, currently use graphology for selection purposes, although many try to keep the fact confidential. Nonetheless, most British selectors remain to be convinced of the method's usefulness – with good reason.

A person's handwriting style is reasonably stable, to the extent that it is usually recognizable as belonging to a particular individual even with slight variations dictated by mood or circumstances (see Figure 9.1). Because of this stability, graphologists often make assertions about the relationship between specific features of handwriting and personality. The specific features of handwriting used by graphologists, when assessments are made, include the slant, size, width, regularity, pressure, loops and the style of connecting letters. These are thought to reveal strengths, weaknesses and even hidden motivations. It is difficult to believe, however, that an applicant's honesty, intelligence, disposition, loyalty, etc., can be assessed on the basis of these features without a large degree of faith, as there are so

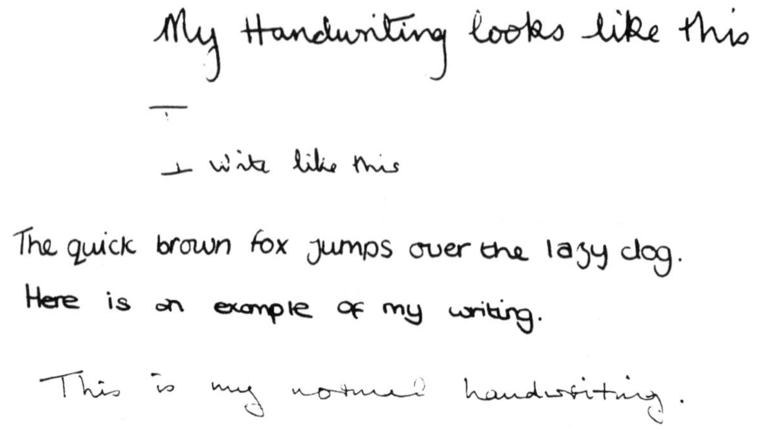

My Handwriting looks like this

I write like this

The quick brown fox jumps over the lazy dog.
Here is an example of my writing.

This is my normal handwriting.

Figure 9.1   Different handwriting styles

many intervening factors that may affect someone's handwriting
style: for example, the way people have been taught to write, fatigue,
laziness or whether the writing is being used for evaluation purposes,
such as when application blanks are completed.

The 'holistic' graphology method focuses on both the applicant's
handwriting and the content of the text as a whole, rather than just
the individual features. In most graphological selection situations,
however, the text content is usually a brief autobiographical account
of the applicant, which may reveal more useful information about
someone than their handwriting *per se*. The scientific evaluations of
graphology that have been conducted lend very little empirical
support to the assertions made for graphology. For example, Zdep
and Weaver (1967) found that graphologists failed to predict the
performance of insurance salesmen. Similarly, Klimoski and Rafaeli
(1983) found that graphologists' predictions about estate agents were
unrelated to supervisory ratings or to actual sales figures. They also
report that two graphologists who independently analysed the same
handwriting samples did not agree very well about the writers'
personalities. More recently Edwards and Armitage (1992) from the
British Broadcasting Corporation (BBC) conducted two experiments. They got four leading UK graphologists to assign handwritten
scripts to groups with contrasting personality or occupation: good or
bad secretaries, highly successful or not-so-successful business

people, actors/actresses and monks/nuns. On average, they were able to do so with 65 per cent of the scripts. One control group of assessors, using *typed* versions of the scripts, were successful with 54 per cent of the scripts. A second control group of lay assessors, using the handwritten scripts, were successful with 59 per cent. The second experiment was conducted with six writers with contrasting personalities and three graphologists. The authors concluded that in both experiments the graphologists had failed to substantiate their claims and support the validity of graphology.

These two studies support previous findings that when non-graphologists are used as control groups, they either achieve the same validities or outperform them. Ben-Shakhar et al. (1986) conducted two studies and found that trained graphologists were no better at predicting an applicant's performance than people who had not been trained, or were no better than would be expected by chance. Similarly, Neter and Ben-Shakhar (cited in Ben-Shakhar, 1989), in a meta-analysis of seventeen published studies, found that the average correlations between inferences of content-laden scripts and the criteria ranged between 0.14 and 0.19 for all judges. Professional graphologists were found to be no better than lay people, but, more surprisingly, psychologists without graphology training were consistently more accurate, and obtained better validities. The authors attributed the small validities obtained in the meta-analysis to the possibility that useful information was provided in the scripts and that this information influenced the assessments. When neutral scripts were used in the studies, the validities of graphologists' predictions were almost zero.

The evidence in favour of graphology for predicting an applicant's job performance is, therefore, poor: so poor, in fact, that a recent report issued by the British Psychological Society (1993), based on thirty years of published research on the use of graphology for selection, concluded that 'graphology is not a viable means of assessing a person's character or abilities'. Similarly, a more recent investigation by the Institute of Personnel Management (now the Institute of Personnel Development) was 'unable to discover any scientific evidence which proves the validity of graphology as a predictor of personality' (IPM, 1994). This evidence suggests that where graphology is used in any part of the selection process, unsuccessful applicants will have a very strong case for pursuing litigation – perhaps even more so, if it comes to light that these assessments have been made without the applicants' knowledge, which is an unethical and objectionable practice.

ASTROLOGY

We all have some knowledge of astrology, perhaps from referring to 'horoscope' predictions printed in newspapers, magazines and books. In most instances, because these horoscopes appear plausible, some credibility is attached to them, although the majority of people view them as a bit of fun, and do not take them too seriously. Others, however, are convinced by them, and run their lives accordingly – hence, the use of astrology in the workplace. Although a small number of executive-search companies in the UK use astrology for selection purposes, in general less than 1 per cent of applicants are selected in this way.

Horoscopes
ARIES

This month is likely to be enjoyable, though there is a tendency for relationships with others to be low-key and even hostile early on. This is not likely to lead to long-term difficulties. As the month progresses various opportunities will open up. Even if there seems to be some risk you should go ahead, as things will work out right in the end.

LIBRA

Your concern about justice will be put to good use in the coming weeks. Someone else is going to feel hard done by and you will need to help put this right. Take care that getting involved here doesn't interfere with your own needs and good relationships with others.

Astrological predictions for selection purposes differ somewhat from those provided in newspapers and the like (see above), because they are individual predictions based on the place, date and time of birth of the applicant. These predictions are based on the rationale that in some meaningful way the position and movements of the stars and planets at birth determine our personality and behaviour. Intuitively, the rationale that our behaviour and personality are determined by the planets seems implausible. Every individual born in the same hospital at the same time should behave in the same way and have similar personalities. Similarly, identical twins should also behave in the same way and have the same personality. Clearly this is not the case (as one of the authors knows from personal experience). And yet! A study conducted by Mayo et al. (1977) indicated that more introverts are born in 'even-numbered' months, and more extroverts are born in 'odd-numbered' months. This result was supported in a further study conducted by a French psychologist, Michel Gauquelin, and colleagues (1979). Gauquelin conducted a series of well controlled and documented studies which examined the links between astrological characteristics and people's occupations, characters and sporting abilities and obtained some positive statistical relationships between them (see Gauquelin, 1978, 1980). For example, in comparison to a randomly selected control group, 500 very eminent French medical practitioners were more likely to have been born when Mars or Saturn had just risen, or just passed the midheaven. Gauquelin obtained similar results linking occupation with planetary positions for successful artists and scientists. Although Gauquelin's studies provided some statistical support in favour of astrology, others have suggested that, because occupations tend to attract people with similar personalities and these personality types are more successful in certain occupations than others, membership of an occupational group explains the statistical relationships (Eysenck and Nias, 1982). Another perspective argues that self-fulfilling prophecies may account for some of the relationships reported. However, the link between astrology and personality is so poor that a prize of £500 offered in 1979 for valid scientific evidence of the purported relationship remains unclaimed.

REFERENCES

In essence, references are intended to fulfil two separate functions: first, to verify the accuracy of information already provided by an applicant; second, based on character judgements and information about a candidate's previous work performance, references are used to predict how well the applicant will perform in the job. References are based on the premise that those who know the candidate are the best source of potentially useful information. Often, however, unless the reference request is in a structured format, decisions about the appropriate information to furnish are left to the referee's discretion. Similarly, the recruiter has a large amount of decision latitude when assessing and weighting the significance of the information provided. References are, therefore, highly subjective and open to error and abuse, particularly as the flow of information is between two people who are unlikely to meet and about an applicant who will never know what was written.

Despite this subjectivity and potential abuse, the use of references in the selection process is widespread in the UK – a trend that appears to be on the increase. For example, surveys indicated that in 1986 references were used by 68 per cent of organizations recruiting less than ten managers a year, and by 50 per cent of organizations recruiting large numbers. In 1992 it was reported that 74 per cent of organizations *always* used references, while in 1993 a survey found that 88 per cent of executive-recruitment consultancies used them. Muchinsky (1979) reported that, although 75 per cent of American companies used references, none of them evaluated their effectiveness in predicting performance. The situation in the UK is unlikely to be different, perhaps because, in many cases, references are used for verification purposes, after an offer of employment has already been made, rather than being used to influence employment decisions. When references are requested after selection decisions, they are intended to provide a final check on the suitability of the applicant, usually in terms of their honesty, cooperativeness and social adjustment. (When used for this purpose, organizations may find integrity tests a more valid option.) One practical reason why references are often used to verify information supplied by the applicant after a job has been offered is that those already in employment may not wish their present employer to know that they are seeking employment elsewhere. If the recruiting organization insisted on references prior to the selection process, this might reduce the applicant pool. At the very least, good candidates may refrain from applying. For those companies recruiting junior clerical and secretarial levels or those with limited resources, it may not be cost-effective to use more refined selection methods. In these circumstances, references appear to be a particularly attractive proposition as they are cheap to obtain (i.e. it only takes one letter and a few stamps, and other people assess the applicant without expecting payment).

Although surveys reveal extensive use, the available research investigating the psychometric properties of references shows that their reliability is disappointing. If what is being said about applicants is reliable, we would expect different referees to say the same type of things about the applicant. However, early researchers found a negative correlation between references provided by supervisors and by acquaintances, although small positive correlations (0.24) were found for those given by a combination of co-workers and supervisors with acquaintances. Similarly, others obtained reliability estimates of about 0.17 for references provided for would-be administrative law judges. More recent work by Mosel and Goheen (1982), with 904 applicants for nine different jobs, obtained reliability estimates ranging from 0.01 to 0.98, with 80 per cent of them being less than 0.40. This evidence suggests that different referees focus on different facets of applicants' behaviour. Indeed, Baxter et al. (1981) found that referees have their own habitual ways of describing others. Because of this, there is likely to be more agreement in the way the same referee describes different applicants, rather than agreement between different referees about the same candidate.

If the reliability of references is low, the same can be said for validity. During the 1980s researchers showed that the predictive validity of the reference is not very good. The average validity coefficient appears to be about 0.14. Validities above 0.2 are a rare phenomenon. Different groups of researchers have concluded that 'because of low reliability, leniency error and poor response rates by previous employers, only a certain segment of the applicant population will have meaningful references available, unless special and costly procedures are undertaken'. Others suggest that the validity and reliability of references can be improved if a *structured* format is provided, *and* the information sought *matches criterion behaviours*. Jones and Harrison (1982), for example, in a study of applicants for Dartmouth Naval College, asked head teachers to rate applicants on seven dimensions. Two of the dimensions (sports and extra-curricular activities, and application to studies) correlated with the naval college's ratings of leadership and general conduct, and examination grade, respectively. Moreover, the combined reference rating of all seven dimensions predicted the applicants' 'total selection score' reasonably well. Williams and Dobson (1987) explored a novel way of matching references with criterion behaviours. They invited referees to preview the army officers' selection process, in order to familiarize the referees with the competencies required of applicants. They obtained a correlation of 0.26 between the subsequent reference reports and the applicants' performance during officer training. In most instances, inviting potential referees such as head teachers to review an organization's selection process is impractical and expensive, for both parties. It is not, however, beyond an organization's capabilities to furnish specific information about a job, when requesting a reference. This should ensure, at the very least, that the reference provided will be focused on the particular job characteristics that are important to the recruiting organization.

It is not necessarily the case, however, that references will be provided when requested. If typical research results are anything to go by, the response rate for reference requests will range between 35 and 56 per cent, unless the employing organization makes a concerted effort to follow up requests with telephone or face-to-face interviews. Even when references are provided they are likely to suffer from leniency effects (i.e. they will all be positive), as illustrated in the Rainbow example. This is because most applicants nominate only those they know will provide a good reference. After all, there is not much point in nominating someone who will provide a bad reference! In part the leniency effect may also be due to social norms which dictate that the provision of a bad reference is not the done thing. Rather than giving a bad reference, most would make it quite plain that they do not feel able to write anything positive. In fact, research suggests that reference writers themselves exhibit a tendency to give applicants the benefit of the doubt, by saying only positive things and not being critical. In addition, if an applicant is liked by the referee, it is likely that the reference provided will be longer than if the applicant is disliked. The leniency effect, therefore, is derived from two sources: the applicants, by their choice of referees, and the referees themselves. Leniency effects may partially explain why the reliability and validity of references is low.

Reference reports are used extensively by the majority of organizations, despite their inherent weaknesses. Improvements in reliability and validity can be achieved by providing a structured format that focuses on the characteristics required in the job, and by soliciting facts rather than evaluations.

EDUCATIONAL ACHIEVEMENT

Despite the fact that the majority of employers specify the level of educational qualifications required for a job, the majority of scientific evidence has failed to demonstrate a significant link between educational qualifications and job performance. For example, a meta-analytic review of thirty-five studies found that educational achievement explained only 2.4 per cent of the variance in job performance. Educational achievement is often used as evidence of an applicant's competency or ability. Although some research suggests that those who perform well at school are more mature, able and highly motivated, other research has shown that the number of 'A' and 'O' levels held by recruits (executive officers in the Civil Service) is *negatively* correlated with their overall performance and promotability ratings (Civil Service Commission, 1987), suggesting that less qualified people would have done the job better. Reilly and Chao (1982), in their summary of the predictive validity of educational achievement (Grade Point Average) in the USA, found that qualifications were correlated more closely with salary levels (0.27) than supervisory ratings (0.14), suggesting that educational levels are used to determine applicants' starting salaries. Not surprisingly, however, educational level has been found to correlate reasonably well with training grades.

In the USA the use of educational qualifications for personnel selection has been ruled unlawful in numerous court cases (Merrit-Haston and Wexley, 1983) on the grounds that it unfairly discriminates against minorities. North (1994) very persuasively argued that the same can be found in the UK. For example, due to the fact that the attainment of qualifications has increased year on year since the 1950s, older workers are inevitably discriminated against because many of them do not have formal educational qualifications. Older women in particular are even more disadvantaged, because on average they obtained fewer qualifications than the men. North provided other evidence of discrimination related to educational qualifications on the grounds of race, social class and geographical location, and argued that using qualifications as a crude cut-off point to dissuade applicants results in smaller applicant pools, the quality of which may be less than that of those excluded.

These findings suggest that, in the not too distant future, UK employers wishing to use educational qualifications as selection criteria will have to furnish real evidence that those with higher educational qualifications are significantly better at their jobs than those with lower or no educational qualifications. In the light of the demographic changes occurring in the working population, people excluded from applying for positions or rejected on these grounds may have a very strong case for unfair discrimination if this evidence is not readily available. Some evidence that employers are taking note of this is provided by the Civil Service Commission (1987) report which states: 'The Inland Revenue had at first proposed a sift of external candidates based solely on academic attainment, but this was held to be unfair and impracticable given the diversity of qualifications which entitle their holders to compete for executive officer posts.'

This type of unfair discrimination may be avoided by using job-related qualifications such as City & Guilds, the National Vocational Qualification (NVQ) framework, or competencies appropriate to the level of job applied for. For example, the Management Charter Initiative (MCI) has defined generic national standards of perform-ance for both supervisors and managers. These are comparable to NVQ levels 3, 4 and 5, although at the time of writing the standards for senior managers are still under development. Other important job-related qualifications are awarded by professional bodies, whereby designatory letters are granted after a predetermined period of appropriate experience (e.g. CPsychol denotes a Chartered Psycholo-gist). For selection purposes, the benefits of using these in place of educational qualifications are that people have been assessed and proven to be competent in relation to various features of job performance, and as such they are clearly job-related.

SUMMARY

This brief tour of alternative personnel selection methods has demonstrated a wide range of perspectives that, in the main, are less than useful to organizations. Most of the methods described rely on subjective interpretations, and as such are open to error and abuse. While the use of references is widespread, research has shown that they are not very reliable and their criterion-related validity is suspect. The same can be said for self-assessments, although current research suggests that the concept of self-efficacy holds some promise. Peer assessments are more reliable, and show reasonably good criterion-related validity. They are difficult to obtain for external candidates, and are used mainly for identifying people for promotion or development purposes, although executive search companies often obtain them to ascertain a potential candidate's reputation. The use of educational qualifications as the sole basis for selection is both discriminatory and less than useful, particularly as they do not predict how well people will perform in the job. However, they may provide information about how easily people can be trained, and could be used in conjunction with other selection methods. If qualifications are to be used, it is better to focus on those that are job-related. Fortunately, the use of graphology and astrology in personnel selection is not very common. These methods are extremely suspect and should never be used to select candidates – not least because candidates rejected by their use would have a very strong case for litigation.

10 *Personnel selection decision-making standards*

Wyndham and Waugh had established a powerful reputation as a high-street retailer with very high quality standards. The company had a nationwide network of stores and was a magnet for young, ambitious people who wanted a career in retailing. The graduate recruitment and selection system had been installed four years ago by a team involving external consultants and internal human resources specialists. In outline, the scheme involved four stages:

- an initial sift based on a weighted and scored application form;
- a company visit;
- an assessment centre;
- a final behaviour-based structured interview.

Although line managers had been pleased with the quality of new recruits produced by the scheme for the first few years, it was clear from more recent annual appraisal reports that there were increasing problems with new entrants to the company. These problems were particularly visible in the recently developed Financial Services Division of the company. This division had grown rapidly in recent years and was now taking almost a third of the new graduate recruits to the company. Since the original introduction of the scheme there had been no large-scale evaluation and the scoring procedures had not been revised in any way. From the outset, various elements in the application form, assessment centre and interview had been given different weights when deriving the final score for that stage of the process. For example, in the assessment centre, the assessors rated each candidate's performance on the various exercises and produced scores on a set of five competencies:

- (*M*) motivation to succeed;
- (*I*) interpersonal skills;
- (*C*) commercial acumen;
- (*R*) reliability;
- (*A*) analytical ability.

These competency scores were then combined to produce an overall assessment rating for each candidate. The scores were not combined equally. Because of the strong retailing and customer-contact orientation of the organization, motivation and interpersonal skills were given more weight in the calculation of the final score. The equation used was:

$$\text{Overall rating} = M \times 22 + I \times 3 + C + R + A$$

The recruitment manager for Wyndham and Waugh arranged for some statistical analyses of the previous records to be done. The analyses compared the appraisal ratings given by managers with the scores obtained by candidates on the various selection procedures. The analyses were carried out separately for the Financial Services Division and the Retail Division. In brief, the analyses showed that the overall assessment ratings from the assessment centres were closely related to subsequent performance of recruits in the Retail Division but the overall assessment ratings were not strongly associated with the performance of recruits in Financial Services. Using the statistical procedures of multiple regression analysis the links between the individual assessment competencies were explored. The results revealed that performance in Financial Services was dependent on good performance across all of the assessment-centre competencies and not particularly influenced by commercial acumen and analytical skills. A much more accurate prediction of performance in Financial Services was obtained by simply summing all of the scores from the assessment centre, without giving higher weights to any individual competencies. This practice was adopted in future years whenever candidates were being considered for appointment in the Financial Services Division of Wyndham and Waugh.

The organizational and personal costs of poor personnel selection decisions may be substantial. Chapter 5 of this book has shown how the gains and losses resulting from personnel selection decisions can be estimated. It is clear that a major contribution to the efficiency of most organizations may be gained from good personnel selection and it is equally clear that devastating losses may also occur if poor selection decisions are made. Most of the earlier chapters in this book have concentrated on explaining how individual differences between people can be understood and measured so that personnel selection decisions can be taken. Although there has been extensive coverage of the methods that might be used to take selection decisions there has been no detailed examination of the decision-making process itself. It is obviously important to understand the technical information on the validity of any particular selection method. Consideration of the way in which the method is used, usually in combination with others, to take actual decisions in organizational settings, is also essential. This chapter deals with personnel selection decision-making.

As well as understanding how to use personnel selection methods in organizations it is also important to recognize that personnel selection decision-making procedures are always imperfect. There is no procedure in existence that can ensure good decisions on all cases. This is obvious if consideration is given to the criterion-related validities of personnel selection methods. Validity coefficients of 1.0 (i.e. perfect predictions of candidates' behaviour) are unheard of. Even using a combination of the best methods would be unlikely to produce a multiple validity in excess of 0.7, explaining about half ($0.7^2 = 0.49$) of the variance in candidates' criterion behaviour. The reason for this result is also apparent: stable individual characteristics of candidates, which are really all that can be measured in a selection procedure, are not the sole determinants of any individual's behaviour. Chapter 2 looked in some detail at the ways in which people can differ and also reviewed the influence of situational factors on behaviour. However much we learn about someone at the selection stage it is impossible to predict the effect that situational factors (domestic or work-related) might have on behaviour. In other words, selection procedures can maximize the probability that someone will be successful but the influence of organizational or other situational factors such as job design, supervision, the economic environment or home circumstances ensure that there is considerable uncertainty about how things will work out in each particular case. The diagram in Figure 10.1 provides an illustration of some of the situational factors that are involved in determining behaviour at work, and places the potential gains from personnel selection in context.

MAKING DECISIONS

In most selection situations, information about candidates is available from several sources, usually derived from different selection methods. For example, information from an application form, structured interview results and psychometric test scores may all be

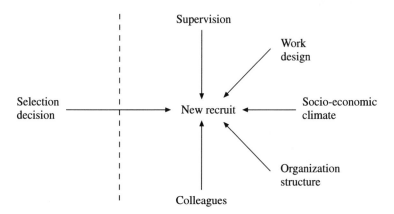

Figure 10.1   Factors involved in determining behaviour at work

available to a personnel manager intending to select a new management trainee. How the information is best used is dependent on many things, the most important of which include the number of posts available, the nature of the job requirements, the validity of the selection methods used, and the expertise of the selection decision-maker.

In a large organization, where there are many posts of the same kind and where statistical monitoring of the validity of the selection procedure is possible, the most sensible way of making decisions will differ from that of much smaller organizations with a single vacant position. When a reasonable amount of statistical information is available it may be possible to develop empirically based cut-off points for each predictor, which can be used to help in decision-making. Figure 10.2 shows how the information on the psychological test scores of candidates collected over a number of years by an organization could be used to derive cut-off scores.

In the diagram in Figure 10.2a, there is a very strong link between the scores on the psychological test and the measure of work performance. This is why the various data points all fall quite close to the best-fit line on the graph. There are well established statistical procedures (regression analyses) which can be used to establish the line of best fit and the magnitude of the correlation between the selection score and the work performance score. In Figure 10.2b, although there is still some link between scores on the test and work performance, the relationship is not as strong. This is again apparent when the location of the best-fit line, in relation to the data points, is examined. At one level, identifying a cut-off point is a simple matter and is done by choosing a score on the work-performance axis that is felt to be the minimum desirable. Then (as shown in Figures 10.2a and b) the point on the other axis associated with this minimum score may be identified by drawing perpendicular lines linking the two axes, via the best-fit line.

Figures 10.2c and d show how the level of criterion-related validity of the selection measure has a major influence on the confidence that should be placed in a cut-off score derived in this way. For Figure 10.2c, where the criterion-related validity (the correlation between the selection test and the work-performance score) is high, the range of work-performance scores that is likely to have been produced by candidates with acceptable selection scores in the example shown in Figure 10.2c is quite narrow. By contrast,

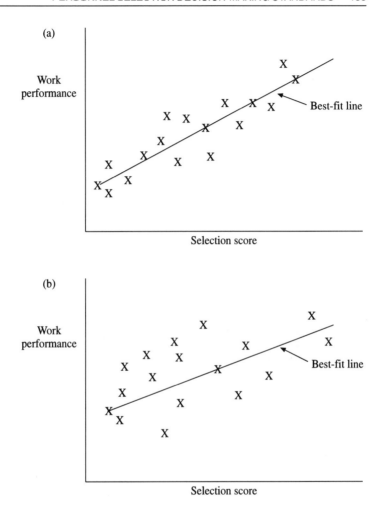

Figure 10.2   Cut-off scores and criterion-related validity

when validity is poorer the range of performance scores from a particular test score is much broader. Quite a few of the people who obtained the cut-off score did not do particularly well at work, several failed to reach the minimum performance standard set earlier. Notice also that several people who fell below the cut-off for the selection test would have been wrongly rejected, since their work performance scores are perfectly acceptable. These diagrams illustrate the general

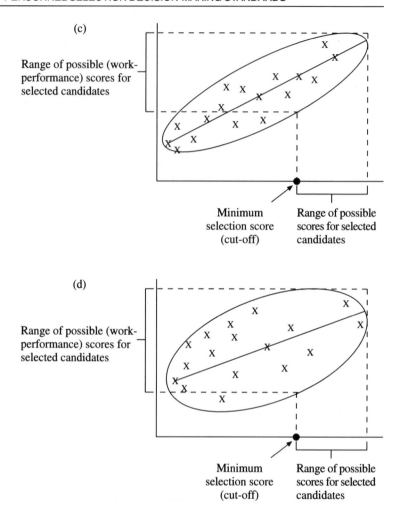

point that selection decisions based on valid selection methods are likely to be better than decisions based on less valid procedures. In particular, cut-off points will produce more selection errors when less valid methods are used. For practical selection decisions this means that the amount of leeway given to candidates in relation to cut-off points needs to take account of the validity of the method on which they are based.

Another important consideration concerns the kind of information carried by each selection method. To illustrate this point, consider how useful it would be to have information about candidates from three different tests of intelligence, compared to one intelligence test, one personality measure and the results of a structured interview. Most selection decision-makers would prefer to have information from the three different sources rather than the results from three intelligence tests. Although intelligence tests are generally reliable, there would be little to be gained from having three separate estimates from three separate tests. Selection methods that provide unique information about candidates are the best ingredients in any battery of measures. As the example given above illustrates, there is little benefit in obtaining the same information about candidates from different methods. Obviously, in reality, the situation is rarely as clear-cut as the example, and few people would consider using three intelligence tests together. Selectors do, however, use interviews, personality tests and references as part of the same selection process. There is almost certain to be some degree of overlap in the information obtained from these methods and it is important, in any selection procedure, to ensure that the collection of redundant information is minimized. For example, a loosely structured interview, a general personality inventory and an open-ended reference request asking about candidates' personal characteristics could produce a great deal of redundant information. By contrast, an intelligence test, a personality test and a structured interview could provide much more useful and thorough information; Figure 10.3 illustrates this. The question of how much emphasis to place on information from different methods lies at the heart of selection decision-making. Different strategies may be used to combine information, including the use of 'clinical' or statistical methods, multiple hurdles and multiple regression techniques.

Using a clinical method involves the decision-maker in using his or her judgement and experience to combine the information about candidates; by contrast the statistical approach makes use of numerical weightings and decision rules to combine the information. There are arguments for and against both approaches, but, in general, studies have found that the statistical procedure is superior. Obviously, despite the general superiority of statistical methods it is sometimes better for the selection decision-maker to combine information in a softer, more subjective way (i.e. clinically). This might be the case when looking at candidates for very senior or

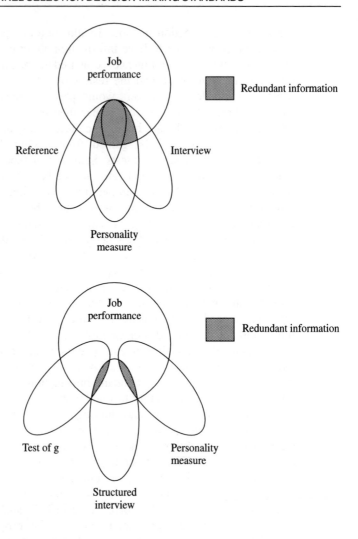

Figure 10.3   Overlapping redundant material from three separate sources of information

unusual positions. In these circumstances there is relatively little hard evidence available that might be used to combine the information. The decision must be based on a clear view of the job requirements (derived from a systematic job analysis). The information about candidates is then balanced and combined to provide an overall evaluation of each candidate's strengths and weaknesses in relation to the job. Often all that is needed is some way of ranking candidates from most to least suitable, although it is also important to be sure that any candidate who might be offered a position is above the minimum standard of competency required for the post. Even when information is being combined by non-statistical methods it is crucial that the decision be based on job-relevant information, which is evaluated as objectively as possible. Combining information by clinical approaches should still produce selection decisions that are based on factors that, as far as possible, can be shown to be directly related to subsequent success in the job. Of course, when dealing with unique positions, there will be little or no hard evidence of what contributes to overall job success. In a way this makes it even more important to remain focused on job relevant factors and not be distracted by other features of candidates.

Statistical methods can be applied to selection decision-making most readily in settings where large numbers of candidates are involved and where numerical data on candidates have been collected over a number of years. The most sophisticated statistical approach makes use of multiple regression techniques. The general procedure of statistical regression analysis can be applied to selection situations where one (or more) scores are derived from the selection procedure(s) used. The scattergram in Figure 10.4 shows the scores for a group of current employees on a spatial ability test and ratings of work performance provided by their supervisors. Linear regression analysis provides a statistical procedure for deriving the best-fit line, which is also shown on the figure. This example is similar to the one given earlier in this chapter when the derivation of cut-off scores was discussed.

Like all straight lines on graphs of this sort, the best-fit line may be described mathematically by a simple equation. This equation takes the standard form:

$$Y \text{ (Work-performance score)} = A \times X \text{ (Test score)} + C$$

The work-performance score (Y) is equal to the score on the test (X) multiplied by a regression weight (A) plus a constant (C). The function of regression analysis is to derive values for A and C. For example, the values of A and C for the data in Figure 10.4 could be

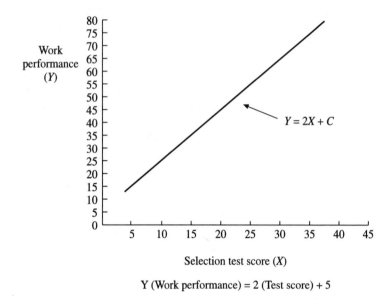

Y (Work performance) = 2 (Test score) + 5

Figure 10.4   Using linear regression analysis to predict work performance

found to be $A = 2$, $C = 5$. The formula for predicting work performance would then become:

Work performance = 2 (Test score) + 5

A test score of 14 would thus be expected to produce a work-performance score of 33.

In many selection settings, more than one score is available for each candidate and *multiple* regression analysis provides a way of deriving the regression weights for each of the available scores. What this means is that for any selection procedure it is possible to derive a precise equation that will give the best possible prediction of any candidate's future work performance. An illustration of such an equation is:

Work-performance score = 2.5 × (Score on test 1)
+ 3 × (Score on interview) + 25

The examples given above provide a clear view of why the statistical method is usually superior to clinical judgement; when a specific formula is available to give the *best available* estimate of each candidate's future work performance, no other method, such as clinical judgement, is capable of doing any better. As the Wyndham and Waugh example illustrates, it is important to monitor and, if necessary, revise weights for different elements in a selection procedure.

Even when there is not enough information available to derive an empirically based regression equation, it may still be best to provide specific numerical weights for each separate score obtained from the selection method. This will ensure that everyone involved in the selection process gives equal weight to the same information about candidates. Equally, it is important not to allow any numerical scoring system, especially if it is not empirically based, to override common sense or to impose unhelpful constraints on selection decision-makers.

MULTIPLE CUT-OFF AND MULTIPLE HURDLES

An example of when it is sensible to override the guidance provided by simple weighted scoring systems arises when a poor score on one of the selection criteria cannot be counterbalanced by a good score on another. This might occur if a minimum level of competency in a particular sphere is needed. It may be, for instance, that a candidate for a job as a bilingual secretary must have a minimum level of competency in two languages. No amount of extra ability in shorthand or typing skills could make up for a lack of language ability. In such a case a multiple cut-off strategy would be adopted in which minimum standards in some areas would need to be attained before a candidate could be considered in overall terms.

A related technique involves the use of multiple hurdles when candidates are required to satisfy a series of requirements in sequence. The fundamental principle operated here is to use the least time-consuming and least expensive hurdles to eliminate candidates early in the process, so that most time may be allocated to detailed evaluation of the most promising candidates. It is essential here to ensure that the methods used in the early stages have high validity, otherwise good candidates may be rejected in error at too early a stage. One of the best procedures to use in the early stages of a multiple hurdles procedure is biodata (see Chapter 8).

ILLUSIONS AND ERRORS IN SELECTION DECISIONS

If asked, most people would probably claim reasonable confidence in their ability to use information well and arrive at unbiased decisions. Unfortunately the evidence from research in cognitive psychology has revealed that people are prone to certain very consistent errors when making judgements and decisions. One of the most pervasive errors is known as 'the fundamental attribution error' (Nisbett and Ross, 1980; Ross and Anderson, 1982). This concerns a tendency to attribute the causes of other people's behaviour to them as individuals, rather than to the situational factors that may have caused them to behave as they did. In one classic experiment people were asked to make judgements about the positions that essay writers took on specific controversial issues. Even when they were told that the essay writers had been requested to argue a particular case, judges inferred that the views expressed in the essays were in line with the writers' personal characteristics.

This attributional error can cause particular problems in selection settings. An interviewer may infer that a candidate who has been made redundant must have been one of the weaker employees, when in fact the redundancy had nothing to do with his or her personal abilities. The error arises because often all that we are aware of is how other people behave; we cannot see the forces that are acting upon them. There is no simple way of avoiding the fundamental attribution error but it is obviously important to be aware of it and seek to guard against it.

Perhaps even more likely to contaminate personnel selection decisions is an error known as 'framing bias' (Tversky and Kahneman, 1988; McNeil et al., 1988). McNeil et al. (1988) presented people with identical information contained in negative and positive frames as follows.

- Survival frame

Of 100 people having surgery, 90 will live through the surgery, 68 will be alive at the end of the first year, and 34 will be alive at the end of five years.

Of 100 people having radiation therapy, all live through treatment, 77 will be alive at the end of the first year, and 22 will be alive at the end of five years.

- Mortality frame

Of 100 people having surgery, 10 will die during treatment, 32 will have died after one year, and 66 will have died after five years.

Of 100 people having radiation therapy, none will die during treatment, 23 will die after one year, and 78 will die after five years.

In the survival frame (positive for surgery), the percentage of people who preferred radiation to surgery was 18 per cent. In the mortality frame (negative for surgery), 47 per cent of people preferred radiation to surgery. In fact, both frames provide exactly the same information!

A selection decision-maker who is concerned about the serious consequences of making a poor choice may be preoccupied with the negative consequences of getting the wrong person. This would focus attention on the negative aspects of candidates and provide the decision-maker with a negative frame. This might well explain why some research has shown that interviewers pay more attention to negative information about candidates (London and Hakel, 1974). Brodt (1990) provides a clear review of the decision biases mentioned above and gives examples of how they may be important in personnel selection practice.

It is important to remember that candidates, as well as organizations, are involved in the personnel selection decision-making process. When preferred candidates do not accept job offers the organization suffers. The personnel selection process is the first stage of a relationship between a person and an organization that may last for many years, and it is important that the feelings and needs of candidates are given due consideration. Features of selection procedures such as realistic job previews can have an important role to play in ensuring that candidates make the right decision about whether or not to accept an employment offer. Throughout the selection process it is important that candidates gain an accurate impression of the organization and job in question.

SUMMARY

Making personnel selection decisions involves the use of all available sources of information about the candidates. This chapter has explored the major ways in which information may be combined to provide a basis for making selection decisions. The use of valid selection methods is an important prerequisite for good selection decision-making. Clinical judgement and statistical scoring procedures may both be used to make selection decisions, though there is some evidence of the general superiority of statistical approaches. Psychological research has revealed that people are prone to several consistent types of errors when making decisions. Selection decision-making may be adversely affected by the general errors of judgement.

11 *Continuous improvement*

There are several future developments in the psychological issues linked to personnel selection that are worth attention. In very broad terms these are concerned with technical factors concerning the selection methods themselves, the relationship between candidates and organizations, and the practical problems confronting selection decision-makers in organizations.

CANDIDATES AND ORGANIZATIONS

Psychologists have identified an important distinction between two different kinds of justice. Procedural justice concerns the fairness of how something is done, whereas distributive justice is concerned with how things are shared between people. Both kinds of justice are important in personnel selection. Research mentioned earlier in this book showed how the adequacy of a selection procedure may have an impact on how candidates react to the procedure and the organization responsible. The way in which a selection procedure is conducted is an indication to participants of the level of procedural justice involved. A candidate who is not well qualified but knows that he or she can outperform much better qualified people, will not feel that a high level of procedural justice is present in a selection system that concentrates on qualifications and does not investigate candidates' potential to do the job. New graduates may feel disadvantaged by a system that requires them to conduct work-sample tests alongside candidates with several years' work experience but no degree. As far as distributive justice is concerned, this is most relevant when the outcomes of personnel selection and assessment processes become known. Candidates may often feel badly served by a process that seems to provide better results for certain groups (e.g. Oxbridge graduates, white people, men).

The changing nature of society is certain to be reflected in personnel selection practices. One inevitable development will be that candidates will be more and more inclined to challenge procedures that they see as unjust. Sometimes they will be assisted in these challenges by official bodies set up to ensure fairness. Throughout this book we have stressed the need for selection procedures to be accurate (i.e. valid and reliable). The accuracy of a selection procedure is closely linked to the apparent fairness of the procedure. The use of valid methods does not guarantee that candidates will see the system as just, but the use of arbitrary and partial selection procedures is increasingly likely to be challenged by candidates or organized bodies. What these developments mean is that organizations will be under increasing pressure to make use of selection procedures that are technically and morally sound – and can be shown to be so. American psychologists are accustomed to visiting courts to explain, defend or attack specific selection systems that are the subject of dispute. We can expect this to be a growing trend in other countries. The justice embodied in a selection process is likely to be of relevance in a legal, employment relations context. The justice of a selection or assessment process is also important when issues of employee attachment and career development are considered. This aspect is of special importance when within-organization assessment procedures are being employed. There is an increasing expectation amongst members of most organizations that they can expect to be treated in a transparently fair and equitable fashion. Selection and assessment procedures that do not meet this expectation will increasingly be negatively regarded by organizational members.

PERSONAL CONSEQUENCES OF SELECTION AND ASSESSMENT

Earlier sections of this book have made it clear that the financial costs and benefits to the organization of personnel selection can be estimated. The financial gains and losses for individuals are reasonably apparent (at least when the narrow issue of getting a job or being rejected are considered). The psychological consequences of assessment, feedback and success or failure for individual candidates represent a further important area for consideration. The traditional personnel selection system seems to operate on the assumption that assessment is a psychologically neutral process that does not exert a powerful influence on people. Models of selection and assessment do not generally include consideration of the effects that assessment might have on candidates (see Hesketh and Robertson, 1993 for an exception to this). Everyday experience in organizational settings reveals that assessment can be a very demanding and psychologically demanding process that is far from neutral for the candidates concerned. This is often particularly striking when internal assessment and placement procedures are concerned. Candidates may become very anxious about the outcome of the process but even more importantly they may develop strong emotional reactions and views about the organization that influence their future behaviour. For example, it is quite reasonable to expect that candidates who fail to obtain their goal (e.g. placement on a 'fast track' or promotion) will lose some commitment to the organization. Negative outcomes of this type may be especially likely if candidates also feel that the assessment procedures used were inadequate in some way.

In recent years the issue of the psychological impact of assessment and selection procedures on candidates has been investigated in a small number of research projects. This research (see Fletcher, 1991; Robertson et al., 1991; Iles and Robertson, in press) is beginning to clarify the key issues and concepts that are involved. Some of the research has shown that assessment and selection experiences may have an effect on various psychological characteristics such as self-esteem, job satisfaction, or work attitudes such as commitment to the organization. There is too little research for findings to be given with any confidence, but there is sufficient evidence to conclude that organizations should pay attention to the impact that assessment and selection experiences may have on individuals. Obviously there is a problem here for organizations in that there is no point in using assessment methods that do not produce different performance levels amongst candidates. The purpose of such procedures is generally to identify candidates' strengths and weaknesses and often to select people for specific organizational roles; not everyone can be successful, otherwise there would be no point in using the procedures. On the other hand, organizations do run the risk of having a negative impact on existing employees who are not successful. These problems are clearly less troublesome if the assessment is being conducted for development purposes only, though there is still the potential for feedback to exert some positive or negative effect.

To examine what organizations might do to minimize the potential negative impact of assessment procedures it is important to distinguish between the decision itself (promotion or fast-track development etc.), the way in which the decision is arrived at and the career consequences of the decision. Obviously not all decisions can be in the candidate's favour and a negative decision may well have unavoidable negative effects. There is some evidence from research (Robertson et al., 1991) which suggests that the *way* in which the decision is made may help to multiply or reduce its impact. It also seems that the candidate's view of the consequences of the decision on his or her career may also affect the psychological impact of the decision. Some of the variables that might be involved in determining psychological impact are as follows:

- candidates' beliefs about the adequacy of the system;
- intrusiveness of the method;
- face validity of the method;
- apparent relevance of the selection method to the job;
- candidates' characteristics, e.g. career stage, personality, work involvement;
- candidates' beliefs about the career impact of the assessment;
- quality and accuracy of feedback to candidates.

What this emphasizes is that, although there is likely to be some unavoidable impact from a negative decision, other features of the assessment will also determine how a candidate reacts. It is at least theoretically possible that a candidate could perform badly in an assessment but experience no negative impact. This might happen if the candidate felt very confident that the assessment procedure was valid and he or she was given sensitive, development-oriented, accurate feedback. There are several actions that might be taken to ensure that the impact of selection and assessment procedures is as benign as possible.

- use valid selection procedures;
- use methods that are transparent (i.e. candidates are aware of each method and why it is used);
- brief candidates about the validity and aims of the methods used;

- provide post-assessment feedback (by a trained person) and counselling, if possible;
- ensure that the organization and its reward systems value solid performers, as well as high-fliers.

These actions are clearly important since it would be utterly pointless for an organization to identify (quite accurately, perhaps) people for accelerated development or promotion at the expense of alienating or demotivating the remainder of the workforce.

As well as having expectations about the kinds of procedures used in selection processes, candidates are likely also to expect that information collected about them will be available for inspection, scrupulously accurate and stored in a safe, secure place. Many organizations currently hold information about their employees that is sometimes used to assist with placement and selection decisions. In some cases this information is not derived from sound methods and may contain evaluative statements about candidates that would be difficult to justify. Freedom of access to these kinds of information bases is likely to increase, in line with similar developments in all areas of society. Organizations need to ensure that the information held meets the reasonable expectations mentioned above.

In line with the other developments noted earlier, the processes involved in personnel selection are certain to become much more interactive, allowing a greater role for candidates. It is inevitable that, subject to labour market conditions, candidates will be involved in the selection process on a more equal footing than in the past. Personnel selection practitioners can capitalize on this change by using methods that provide candidates with accurate information about the job and the organization, enabling candidates to make informed decisions about how well they fit with the job demands.

TECHNICAL FACTORS

Information technology has already made an impact on the procedures used for psychological assessment (see Bartram, 1994). So far the most visible impact is in the area of psychometric testing. Many contemporary tests of personality and ability can now be administered, scored and, in some cases, interpreted by computer. The computer administration and scoring of psychometric tests is likely to develop and mirror the general increased use of computer technology in everyday life. This is a predictable and uncontroversial development. The British Psychological Society has laid down criteria for computer versions of psychometric tests and will no doubt continue to monitor and facilitate the development of professional computer-based tests.

The much more controversial development concerns the use of computers to *interpret* the results of psychometric tests. Sophisticated 'expert system' software that models the decision-making and diagnostic procedures used by human experts has existed for some time and was employed initially to model the thinking processes of experts in medical and other fields. In a relatively short space of time the use of this kind of software had been imported into psychological testing, and systems began to be developed that could produce narrative reports to describe the psychological characteristics of people. Typically the system is fed with test scores and then uses a series of decision rules and interpretative strategies to generate a written report. The report is generally built up from the test scores. Preset phrases or individual comments are linked together selectively to provide a continuous narrative report. The quality of this final report depends upon several factors. First, the original test on which the report is based needs to be psychometrically sound. However well designed an expert system might be, it cannot produce a good report from a test that lacks reliability or validity. Next, the fidelity of the decision rules in the expert system is important. If these rules produce statements about candidates that are untrue or unjustified, in the light of the original scores, the report will be poor and lack validity. Finally, the complexity and sophistication of the rules and strategies guiding the system will help to determine the overall quality of the report. It is relatively easy to produce an accurate (i.e. high-fidelity) report from a set of test scores by commenting separately on each of the personality scales in the test and drawing on a predetermined phrase for each point on each scale. There would, however, be no variation across candidates for scales where they obtained the same scores, and the reports would be predictable and repetitive. Most important of all, the consequences of combinations of various personality constructs would be ignored completely. This is where the interpretative skill of a professional comes in and where the person being tested is likely to gain most insight into his or her character. A system that is insufficiently complex in this respect is going to provide little gain over the simple viewing of test scores for each scale. Quite a large number of computer-based test interpretation (CBTI) systems have been developed and are readily available to users of psychometric tests. Most test publishers have developed systems for their own tests. In addition to this, there are many other systems, developed independently of the test publishers, that may be used to interpret their products.

Unfortunately knowledge of computer systems design is quite separate from knowledge of psychometrics and psychological theory. Anyone with systems design skills can develop a CBTI system. The consequence of this is that many systems on the market lack the essential properties for the production of a high-quality interpretation. They may be based on poor tests, incorporate inadequate decision rules, use unsophisticated interpretative strategies, or sometimes suffer from all three flaws. The unsophisticated user is extremely vulnerable to well-presented but essentially bogus systems. The simple solution is to consult a Chartered Psychologist for an evaluation of the system and check that the test on which it is based meets the requirements for any psychological measurement procedure, as explained in Chapter 2.

Despite these difficulties the role of new technology in psychological assessment is certain to grow. As well as systems for administering and interpreting tests, the whole process of testing may eventually be revolutionized by the capacity of computers to capture and respond to information. In the ability-testing domain, for example, computer-based tests (CBTs) have the capacity to store and learn from the answers provided by candidates. The information captured in this way can be used to design much more sophisticated testing strategies, built on information about the fine detail of many candidates' responses. The information can also be used, while a specific candidate is still being tested, to tailor the assessment process more closely to his or her abilities and derive a quicker or more detailed analysis. So far, the potential of the computer to revolutionize testing has not yet been realized and there are very few commercial applications of the kind of adaptive testing systems described above. There is little doubt that, in due course, such systems will become routine. For the selection specialist the key will be to select the right point to invest heavily in complex CBTs.

Although progress is not yet going at breakneck speed there are already many examples of interesting new assessment procedures, not directly involving psychometric tests. Bartram (1994) lists several, including one procedure called MAILBOX (Horn, 1991), which is a computerized in-tray exercise showing little duplication of the information provided by tests of personality and ability but good correlations with measures of job success. Another procedure described by Bartram is a test for diver orientation which involves 'swimming' through a virtual three-dimensional maze. Developments of this kind are sure to continue and will provide a range of new selection methods. Many of these will have advantages but all will need to be carefully evaluated to ensure that they are an improvement on what is already available.

Psychologists' theoretical and practical work is also likely to contribute to the development of improved selection procedures. In particular, improved understanding of the role of personal and situational factors in the determination of behaviour will be of value to personnel selection. It is already clear that the design of the work that people do (Wall and Martin, 1987) and the general circumstances in which they live and work have key roles to play in influencing their work-related behaviour and attitudes. At the moment the practical ceiling on the magnitude of validity coefficients for selection methods is about 0.5. In some circumstances combining the information from different methods will produce enhanced validity coefficients but it is generally beyond the expectations of most researchers and practitioners to produce validities much in excess of 0.5. One certain reason for this was discussed in Chapter 2 and alluded to in the previous section: the influence of situational factors (i.e. what happens to people during their life, at both work and home). The inter-relationships between personal characteristics, situational features and behaviour are immensely complex and much of the research effort in contemporary psychology is directed towards unravelling the relationships involved here. As our understanding of these interactions develops so will our capacity to predict someone's behaviour at work.

DEVELOPMENT NEEDS

Personnel selection has progressed well in recent years and the findings of research have had an increasingly marked and rapid impact on practice. It seems likely that the link between research and practice will continue. Both practitioners and researchers will benefit from this. Much of the actual work conducted in organizations is not done by one person working entirely alone. More often than not people are required to coordinate their efforts and to collaborate in the attainment of shared objectives. In some settings this requires people to work together in close-knit teams, whereas in others a looser interaction is needed. The relationships between the people and the extent to which they communicate effectively and support each other is obviously an important ingredient in the overall success of the activities. What this means, of course, for personnel selection, is that one is attempting to predict either how a particular person will fit into an existing setting or how a group of different individuals will work together. Almost without exception the validation research described in earlier chapters of this book has involved the search for links between selection methods and various features of individual work behaviour. The work behaviour in question has usually been related to organizationally relevant indicators of effectiveness such as performance, absenteeism or turnover. Two key features of this work, the focus on *individual* behaviour and the focus on indicators of *effectiveness*, are likely to become less dominant in personnel selection practice. The conventional personnel selection approach, concentrating, as it does, on individual measures, neglects at least some of the issues involved here. The environment into which a new recruit needs to fit can be captured, to an extent, in the job analysis. However, while job analysis may identify that the person needs to work with others it will generally be silent about who these people are and what kinds of characteristics they have! This is true despite the fact that close coordination between existing staff and the new one(s) may be needed.

There is a long history of research into groups and group processes (see Argote and McGrath, 1993). Although this work has produced some important findings about how groups function, there is very little conclusive evidence about how people can best be selected for collaborative work, or what kinds of people work well or badly together. Part of the reason for this lack of helpful research is that some very difficult problems need to be resolved before any useful findings could emerge, some of these being related to the conduct of the research itself (e.g. getting hold of sufficient stable groups to work with). Other problems are of a more conceptual kind and are caused by the fearsome number of variables that might be involved interacting with each other, when even fairly simple questions are asked. Some people have not been put off by the difficulties (e.g.

Belbin, 1981) and have developed theoretical frameworks and associated measurement instruments. These approaches have some promise and certainly provide some access to the awkward and complex issues involved. So far, however, scientific evaluation of such work, particularly the measuring instruments (e.g. Furnham et al., 1993), has revealed weaknesses that require remedying through further development. It seems certain that, over the next decade or so, more and more researchers will turn their attention to the question of how to understand the mixes of personality and ability that make for effective teamwork. The results of this effort should eventually pay handsome dividends in personnel selection practice. For the moment, personnel practitioners will have to continue to make decisions about team membership based on personal experience and judgement, without the benefit of clear research findings.

Linked to the problem of selecting for teams or groups is the practical issue of using several selection methods together. Although this is common practice in organizations too little is known about the overlap in evidence provided by different selection methods. More large-scale research studies are needed to provide clear evidence. For example, although there is clear evidence on the criterion-related validity of both structured interviews and general mental ability tests, the extent to which they measure related or quite distinct constructs is not known. Some researchers have suggested that structured interviews are no more than an oral test of general intelligence (Hunter and Hirsh, 1987); if this is true then they are an extremely cumbersome and costly way of assessing intelligence. Of course structured interviews may provide much more than a measure of intelligence. The point is that we do not know. The same is true of a variety of other selection methods. For example, the links between work-sample tests and intelligence, and those between group exercises and personality, are not well understood. Researchers can be expected to concentrate on the construct validity of many of the major selection methods in the coming years and provide much clearer information about what they measure and where the duplication lies.

One final area where a change of emphasis in personnel selection research and practice might occur concerns the variables chosen as criteria. As noted above, there has been a pronounced tendency for research to focus on effectiveness-related criteria to the exclusion of other variables, such as those related to attachment or well-being. It might well become increasingly common for organizations to be concerned about selecting people who will remain attached to the organization. Selection methods might well be validated against criteria such as employee commitment or even variables that focus on the employees' well-being, such as job satisfaction or psychological health. One reason for this shift might be the increased concern of organizations for the well-being of their members. There is also a strong probability that a desire for protection against lawsuits from distressed employees will encourage organizations to move in this direction.

SUMMARY

In the near future organizations may need to show increasing concern for the impact that selection and assessment procedures may have on people. There is likely to be growing social and legal pressure for selection and assessment procedures to treat people in a fair and positive fashion – without causing them undue negative consequences. The role of information technology is likely to grow, particularly in relation to the administration, scoring and interpretation of psychological tests. Developments are needed in selection methods that can assist with the placing of new recruits into teams or work groups and more knowledge of how various selection methods may be used to complement each other is also necessary.

Appendix A
Norm-based scoring systems

Norm-based scoring systems, of which two types exist, provide a frame of reference with which applicants can be compared to others. Positional scoring systems refer purely to the grading of applicants in relation to others; standardized scoring systems carry information about both the grading of applicants and the magnitude of differences between them. It is important to emphasize that both percentile and standard scores must be used with the relevant reference group. In other words it is nonsensical to compare the scores of student nurses with bank managers.

POSITIONAL SCORING SYSTEMS

The simplest types of positional score are those where an applicant's score is graded as above or below average, or ranked in descending order from best to worst. For example, applicant A stands third on test A, fifth on test B and ninth on test C. However, because ranking depends on the number of people taking the test, when fewer or more people take the test an applicant's placing is likely to change, which makes it difficult to judge meaningfully how well people are performing in relation to others. Other difficulties reside in the fact that an applicants' competency or merit is not reflected in their placing. All the applicants taking the test may be either of a higher or a lower quality than previous groups.

The most refined type of positional score is that of percentile ranks, which attempt to place an applicant in a representative queue, relative to 99 others (see Table A.1). A percentile placing indicates the proportion of other applicants who have scored below the applicant placed on that particular percentile rank. For example, placing applicant A on the 75th percentile indicates that 75 per cent of those taking the test scored worse than applicant A. This is because the system is based on percentile scores that range from nought to one hundred, with nought being the worst and one hundred being the best. In a group of 100 people who each gained a different score, someone with a percentile score of 50 would be placed fiftieth in the queue, while someone with a percentile score of 60 would be sixtieth in the queue. In fact, because of the way in which human characteristics are normally distributed, percentile scales can be misleading unless their meaning is well understood. Consider for example how the scores of 100 people might be spread on a test of numerical ability. Very few people will get extremely high or low scores, and most will be bunched around the middle. The top ten people may have scores from say 80 to 95 (a difference of 15 points). In the middle of the score range, because scores will be bunched together, the 50th percentile might spread from say 47 to 50 (a difference of 3 points). In other words, the difference in percentile terms does not reflect the magnitude of the difference in actual scores. In terms of performance differences the gap between two people at the 90th and 95th percentiles is likely to be much greater than the gap between people at the 50th and 55th percentiles. However, even with this caveat, percentile scores do offer two advantages: an applicant can be compared with all other applicants taking a particular test; and, the same applicants' scores on different

Table A.1 The percentile system

Score	Percentile
64–70	99
62	90
59	80
55	70
54	60
50	50
48	40
46	30
41	20
33	10
0–20	1

tests can be readily evaluated in relation to each other. A major disadvantage resides in the fact that percentile scores do not indicate the magnitude of difference between each applicant's test scores, as they only record the relative achievement of applicants within a particular test.

If a more accurate and meaningful assessment of relative achievement is required it becomes necessary not only to take into account the ranking of applicants but also the size of the differences between them. *Scoring systems based on the normal curve* do exactly that with what are known as *standard scores*. From the properties of a normal curve (see Figure A.1), it is known that one standard deviation (negative or positive) will equate to where 68.26 per cent of all the scores on a test will lie, two will equate to where 95.44 per cent of the scores will lie, and three will equate to where 99.74 per cent of the scores will lie (see Miller, 1984 for a fuller discussion). This property of the normal curve provides a simple way of relating percentiles to candidates' scores so that more meaningful information can be conveyed and is achieved through the use of standard scores.

Standard scores indicate where an applicant's scores lie in relation to the mean score of all the applicants on a particular test (i.e. above or below the mean score), and they show how far the standard score differs from the mean score. These two properties of standard scores simply reflect the two main characteristics of a normal curve: the mean and standard deviation. The mean shows the average score of *all* the applicants on a test, while the standard deviation indicates how much a score differs from the mean score, and as such is a measure of spread.

The simplest type of standard score is a Z score, which simply states how many standard deviations an applicant is above or below the mean. An applicant with a Z score of nought would be exactly on the mean, an applicant with a Z score of minus two (–2) (i.e. a negative score) would be two standard deviations below the mean, and an applicant with a positive Z score of 1.56 would be 1.56 standard deviations above the mean. Converting the raw scores from a test into Z scores is simplicity itself. Just deduct the raw test score from the mean test score, and divide by the amount of spread (i.e. the standard deviation). Most published tests will provide the mean and standard deviation based on norm tables. For example, if a test has a mean of 75 and a standard deviation of 15, an applicant who scored

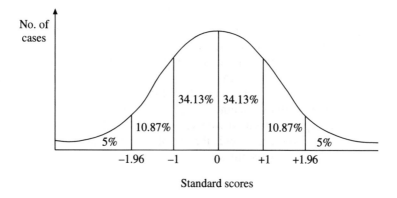

No. of
cases

34.13%   34.13%

10.87%   10.87%

5%   5%

−1.96   −1   0   +1   +1.96

Standard scores

Figure A.1   Standard scores and percentages in the normal curve

90 on the test would have a Z score of 1: that is, (90–75)/15 = 1.
The advantages of using scores based on the normal curve to discriminate between candidates reside in the fact that an applicant can be placed in relation to others while the magnitude of difference between test scores can also be identified. In addition, they avoid distorting or exaggerating the differences between applicants because the magnitude of difference between standard deviations is the same. Thus, the analysis and interpretation of test scores are made somewhat easier.

As noted above, the link between standard scores and percentiles can be exploited to good effect. A standard score of +1 indicates a performance that is one standard deviation better than the mean. As Figure A.1 shows, it is known that in the normal curve a specific percentage of people (84.13 per cent) will obtain a standard score of less than +1 and 15.87 per cent will obtain a better score. In this way standard scores may be interpreted directly into percentile terms and vice versa. For example, to score in the top 5 per cent a candidate needs a standard score of +1.96. Similarly, a standard score of −1.96 would indicate that someone falls in the bottom 5 per cent. A minor disadvantage of standard scores lies in the fact that they include negative and positive signs, as well as decimal points, and these are likely to be left out when copying out results. To avoid this difficulty other types of standard scores may be used by transforming the Z score. In many popular psychological tests such as the 16PF, T scores, stens or stanines are common. A T score adopts a mean of 50, and a standard deviation of 10, with a range from 20 to 80. Sten scores adopt a mean of 5.5 and a standard deviation of 2. The disadvantage of stens resides in the use of half points, and the fact that for those who score the maximum, two digits must be used in computations. Stanines adopt a mean of 5, and are similar to stens except that standard scores are from 0 to 9. Each of these transformed standard scores avoids the use of scores below 0 and may be related directly to percentiles.

Appendix B
Utility analyses

CALCULATING BENEFIT/COST RATIOS

In order to place the benefits expected from good selection procedures in context, it is often useful to provide a point of comparison.
This point is usually derived from estimates of financial gain
expected if the employing organization randomly selected people
without regard to their skills or abilities.

If personnel selection were entirely random and large numbers of
people were recruited, their performance would typically spread out,
with most people performing averagely well in the middle range. The
performance of smaller numbers of people would range from below
average to very poor, with an equally smaller number of people
performing somewhat above average. In other words, as Figure B.1
shows, the performance scores would form a normal bell-shaped
distribution, of which three features are particularly important:

- the centre point of the curve, which represents the mean score (*the mean*);
- the standard deviation (*SD*) which represents the spread of scores from the mean;
- the *ordinate*, which represents the height of the curve at any given point on the bottom axis.

SELECTION RATIO

Good selection, however, depends upon having more applicants than
there are jobs. Indeed, if it were not possible to select from the group
of applicants available, the performance scores of the applicants
would remain in the same distribution as that for selecting people at

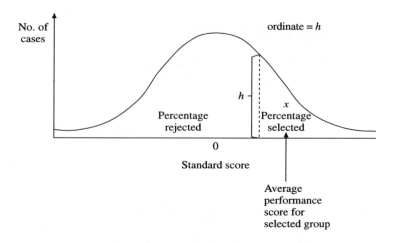

Figure B.1   The mean and ordinate(s) on the normal curve

random. If, however, it were possible to select one applicant in every four (i.e. there are four times as many applicants as jobs available), then some gain can be expected from personnel selection decision-making. In other words, with perfect selection, if the selection ratio was about 0.25 (i.e. the ratio of jobs to applicants), it would then be possible to select the top 25 per cent of applicants on the selection score, and they would also be the top 25 per cent of applicants in terms of their job performance scores (see Figure B.2).

Thus the first feature to focus on when estimating the financial benefits from personnel selection is the selection ratio. If it is necessary to recruit every applicant (i.e. the selection ratio is one), then no gains are possible. Therefore, the more applicants that are available for fewer jobs, the smaller the selection ratio will be and the greater the potential gain to an organization from selecting a small group of good candidates from a larger group of applicants. In essence, therefore, the selection ratio reflects the calibre or quality of those selected, and can be used to determine the cut-off point between accepts and rejects.

Similarly, the selection ratio can be used to estimate the average performance of the successful applicants. (Before attempting to grasp the main points of the next section, the reader should be sure to consult that part of Appendix A which deals with the development of

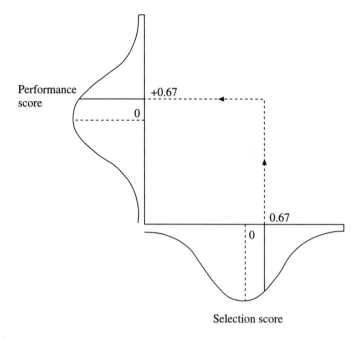

Selection score

Figure B.2   Selection scores and job-performance scores with perfect
selection

'standard scores'.) If the top 25 per cent of candidates could be
identified without error (i.e. if the selection procedure were perfect)
these same people would perform at a similar level on the job. The
average score for any group of normally distributed scores can be
calculated. This is done by dividing the relevant standard score (see
Appendix A) by the height (ordinate) of the unit normal curve at the
point where the standard score lies. Statistical tables will provide the
top 25 per cent of applicants' expected additional performance
output, compared to other applicants, by looking up the relevant
standard score and ordinate. For example, a selection ratio of 0.25
lies at 0.67 standard deviations above the mean, and at this point on
a normal distribution the ordinate would be 0.319. If the ordinate is
then divided by the selection ratio this will provide an indication of
the average performance of those in the relevant band, expressed as
$\bar{Z}_x$, *a standardized performance score*. (The mathematical derivation
of this step is beyond the scope of this book.) With perfect selection,

a selection ratio of 0.25 reveals that the average performance of those selected is 1.28 standard deviations above average (i.e. 0.319/0.33).

CRITERION-RELATED VALIDITY

The selection ratio is not the only factor that influences the benefits of personnel selection. Because perfect selection is rare (as it depends on a perfect relationship between the selection method and the criterion-related measure of work performance), it is necessary to scale down estimates of the average performance output of the successful applicants. Because validity coefficients (See chapter 4) reflect the actual relationship of the selection method to the criterion-measure of work performance, they can be used to scale down predictions of the average output from those selected. If, for example, validity were zero, then even if we selected the top 25 per cent of applicants based on their selection method scores their performance scores at work could be distributed across the whole range with an average at the midpoint of the distribution ($0 = 1.28 \times 0$). If, however, the criterion-related validity of the selection method were 0.5, we would expect that, with a selection ratio of 0.25, the average performance of those selected would be 0.64 standard deviations above average (1.28×0.5). The benefits to be obtained from personnel selection increase in proportion to the validity of the selection method used. Therefore, the better the criterion-related validity of the selection method, the greater the potential financial gain. Obviously, as already explained, if validity were 1.0 (i.e. perfect selection) the average performance of the selected group would be 1.28 standard deviations above average (1.28×1).

MONETARY VALUE

Before the actual financial gains from personnel selection can be estimated, the cash value of one standard deviation (SD_y) in performance has to be calculated. Hunter and Schmidt (1982), on the basis of empirically determined relationships between mean salary and mean work output, proposed that, as a rule of thumb, the monetary value of one standard deviation in job performance (SD_y) was equivalent to between 40 and 70 per cent of the salary related to the job vacancy. However, because conservative estimates tend to be more credible with decision-makers, most applications of this rule of thumb err on the side of caution by using 40 per cent of salary as the benchmark when calculating SD_y. Converting the standard deviation of performance into monetary terms is a simple matter. For example, a starting salary of £14,000 per annum would give us an SD_y estimate of £5,600 p.a. In the previous example, performance improvements were estimated at 0.64 standard deviations. In monetary terms, because SD_y is based on annual salaries, the financial gain would be £3,584 per applicant per year (£5,600 × 0.64). Thus, the added value to the organization from good selection can be considerable.

UTILITY FORMULAE

The complete formula for the financial gain derived from personnel selection can be expressed as:

$$U = (SD_y)(\bar{Z}_x)(r) - C$$

where SD_y is the monetary value of one standard deviation in performance, $\bar{Z}_x$ is the average performance (in standard deviation units) of the selected group (i.e. the standardized performance score), r is the validity coefficient, and C is the costs of the selection procedure. Once all of the parameters have been estimated, it becomes relatively simple to calculate the potential financial gains (ROI) by multiplying each parameter by the other parameters.

However, two further factors also need to be entered in the equation. These are concerned with the numbers of personnel to be selected and the tenure of the recruits once selected. This is because selection systems are rarely used for only one individual and most recruits stay with an organization for some considerable time. Utility estimates need, therefore, to reflect these factors. A worked example is provided below, based on the recruitment of graduates for five management trainee positions:

(a) Assume a selection ratio of 1:4 or 0.25 (the resulting standardized performance score would be 1.28 ($\bar{Z}_x$) standard deviations above average);
(b) assume the selection procedure used psychological tests and situational interviews with a validity of 0.5 (r);
(c) assume the salary for the job is £14K. SD_y equals £5,600, based on the 40 per cent rule;
(d) assume average tenure (T) for existing job holders is 3 years;

(e) assume there are five vacancies (N) to be filled;
(f) assume the total direct costs per applicant (C) are £500.

The financial gain (ROI) per employee per year

$$= (\bar{Z}_x)(r)(SD_y) - C$$
$$= [1.28 \times 0.5 \times £5,600] - £500$$
$$= £3,084$$

The total estimated financial gain (ROI) to the organization of the five management trainees over the next three years

$$= (ROI)(T)(N)$$
$$= \text{Total ROI}$$
$$= £3,084 \times 3 \text{ years} \times 5 \text{ trainees} = £46,260$$

Thus, in this example, each management trainee selected is worth over £3,000 more per year to the organization when compared to selecting people at random. Assuming all five applicants stayed for 3 years, collectively they are worth an extra £46K. A more realistic comparison might be to compare the gains from a proposed new selection procedure with an existing procedure (rather than with selection at random). For example, if unstructured interviews with a validity of only 0.2 were used the gains would be:

ROI $= (SD_y)(Z_x)(r) - C$
$= [1.28 \times 0.2 \times £5,600] - £500$
$= £933.60$ per applicant

Total ROI $= (ROI)(N)(T)$
$= £933.60 \times 5 \text{ recruits} \times 3 \text{ years} = £14,004.00$

Because it is unlikely that an organization would invest in a selection procedure only to use it once and then stop, the selection procedure adopted would be applied to further applicants and would therefore result in much greater returns on investment.

— Glossary of terms

Adverse Impact
This occurs when a selection method produces results that are less favourable to one or more specific subgroups

Aptitude
Refers to someone's potential for achievement in a particular domain, or the possibility of the person being trained to a specified level of ability.

Assessment Centre
A term used to describe a selection process that uses multiple methods and multiple assessors to provide an overall view of a candidate. It does not refer to a geographical location.

Astrology
A pseudoscience that believes that the position of the planets determines people's behaviour and personality.

Behaviourally Anchored Rating Scale
A rating scale consisting of two parts: a clear definition of the characteristic to be rated, and descriptions of overt, observable behaviours reflecting the characteristic. The behaviours are scored at different levels on the scale ranging from what the applicant cannot do to what they can do.

Benefit/Cost Ratio
The proportion of estimated losses or gains expected from pursuing a course of action, in relation to the costs involved.

Biodata	Biographical information detailing an applicant's life history.
Centre Point of Distribution	Represents the mean score (i.e. the mean score of all applicants on a test).
Chartered Psychologist	A professional applied psychologist with the appropriate qualifications and experience, who is on the Register of Psychologists, issued by the British Psychological Society (BPS). Chartered Psychologists have agreed to abide by a Code of Conduct and are accountable to the BPS. Denoted by the abbreviation 'CPsychol'. Expertise in particular areas is denoted by abbreviations (e.g. Occ, Clin, Ed, Foren, Couns) inserted between C and Psychol. Some Chartered Psychologists do not use these abbreviations, even though eligible to do so.
Competency	A person's capacity to demonstrate that they can perform particular tasks or activities to the required standards (e.g. NVQs).
Concurrent Validity	The correlation between scores on a predictor and on a criterion measure obtained at the same time (e.g. the correlation between scores obtained by existing employees on a selection test and their job performance).
Construct Validity	The degree of correspondence between what a test purports to measure and reality. In essence, the body of evidence that supports the idea behind the test.
Content Validity	The degree to which the subject matter of a test matches its intended function and purpose. Test content can be visualized as a sample of items, tasks or behaviours that reflect the domain in question (e.g. an arithmetic test would contain numerical items).
Correlation	A relationship between two (or more) factors,

such that an increase in one is accompanied by a systematic increase or decrease in the other.

Correlation Coefficient

A statistical value that expresses the magnitude of some relationship between two factors (e.g. selection criteria and job performance). The stronger the relationship, the further the coefficient is from zero, with a maximum range from -1 to $+1$.

Cost–Benefit Analysis

A practical way of assessing the desirability of pursuing a particular course of action.

Costs per Applicant (C)

The total direct costs of recruiting and selecting each applicant. Used in personnel selection utility analyses to calculate benefit/cost ratios.

Criterion

A standard against which a judgement or evaluation can be made. In personnel selection, the standard usually reflects some aspect of job performance.

Criterion-based Score

A 'cut-off' score used to indicate an absolute level of performance against certain criteria (e.g. a pass or fail on a driving test).

Criterion-related Validity

The correlation between a selection test and job performance on some specific criterion (e.g. overall performance quality). How closely a test matches *subsequent* performance is defined as the test's *predictive validity*.

Cronbach's Alpha

A reliability coefficient for multiple-item measures that provides an indication of the measure's internal consistency.

Cut-off Score

The score level by which an applicant is deemed to have passed or failed a selection test. Determined by two main features: the *number* and *quality* of applicants required. Its value depends on the criterion-related validity of the test.

Demographics	In personnel selection terms, the distribution of the working population with regards to gender, age, race and socio-economic status and other factors.
Design Cycle Technology	In personnel selection, a framework by which an organization's overall selection procedures, and specific selection methods, can be systematically developed, while taking into account practical as well as technical requirements and constraints.
Evaluative Standards	Standards by which the quality of a measurement system or selection procedure is assessed. Important measurement system standards are reliability, validity, interpretability and practicality. Selection procedure standards include effectiveness, efficiency and benefit/cost ratio.
Face Validity	People's perceptions of how well a test measures what it is supposed to measure.
Faking	Commonly termed 'social desirability', faking refers to the practice of creating a false impression when responding to questions during selection procedures.
Feedback	Information given to candidates about their test performance at the end of a selection procedure, usually in terms of their strengths and weaknesses. Feedback should be constructive.
g	Underlying *general* mental ability that is presumed to be basic to all the specific or special abilities displayed in particular situations. Measured with cognitive-ability tests (e.g. verbal, numerical or spatial).
Graphology	The investigation and study of handwriting. Originally used by forensic specialists to detect written forgeries. Within personnel

selection, a pseudoscience that makes unsubstantiated claims for the value of graphology in assessing candidates' personality.

Integrity Testing   Commonly termed 'honesty testing', and includes the use of 'lie detectors' or 'paper-and-pencil' tests to ascertain a candidate's propensity to indulge in dishonest or disruptive behaviour.

Interpretability   The extent to which the scores on a test are interpretable and meaningful. An important evaluative standard for a measurement system.

Interview   Used in personnel selection to assess the suitability of an applicant. Many forms exist, but only structured methods consistently produce better results.

In-tray Exercise   A 'role-play' exercise, whereby applicants are provided with a basket or file containing letters, memos and other written material and instructed to resolve particular problems.

Job Analysis   A generic term used to denote a methodology for the systematic identification of all the vital features of a job or jobs. This enables personnel specialists to identify their 'customers'' needs and set the necessary standards by which candidates can be assessed.

Job Description   A formal document derived from job analyses that describes the tasks and activities performed by the job holder, as well as the product produced, and also specifies the minimum standards of competence required. Personnel specifications and the criterion by which candidates will be assessed are also derived from the job description.

Job-knowledge tests   A surrogate work-sample selection test designed to assess the amount of job-related information a candidate holds, without the applicant being required to demonstrate job-related behaviours.

Kuder–Richardson Coefficient

A coefficient of internal consistency, normally derived from test-score responses that are dichotomous (e.g. a simple yes/no scoring format).

Leaderless Group Exercises

A 'role-play' group exercise, whereby participants are assessed on social and problem-solving skills. Usually used in assessment-centre selection procedures.

Leniency Effects

The propensity to rate an attribute in a positive manner, regardless of its true state.

Mean Score

The *mean* is the sum of all (e.g. test) scores divided by the total number of scores, and is usually termed the *average* in everyday language. As such the mean is a measure of central tendency.

Mean Square

The average of a set of squared deviations from the mean. In other words, the variance associated with a set of scores.

Meta-analysis

A statistical method for combining the results of many research studies with small sample sizes, to produce findings based on large samples. The method also overcomes problems associated with sampling error and other methodological artefacts.

Multimodal Interview

A type of structured interview that uses multiple methods of assessment. Noteworthy, because it combines the best of situational and patterned behaviour description interviews, in that the questions focus on both past behaviour and future intentions.

Normal Distribution

The theoretically expected bell-shaped probability distribution curve when samples are drawn from a population in which all events are likely to occur. The apex of the curve represents the mean score. The distance from the mean is represented by the standard deviation (68 per cent of scores will always fall within plus or minus one standard deviation).

Norm-based Scoring System

Used to interpret one applicant's score in relation to the scores of other applicants. Often expressed as a percentile or standard score (or both).

Norm Table

A table of numbers by which an applicant's score on a test can be compared to the test scores obtained by similar people. These tables usually include conversions to percentile and standard scores. Developing norm tables requires a minimum of 400 people, and a great deal of care.

Number of Vacancies (V_n)

The number of vacancies the employing organization is attempting to fill. Used in personnel selection utility analyses to calculate benefit/cost ratios.

Patterned Behaviour Description Interview

A type of structured interview where the questions focus on an applicant's past behaviour.

Peer Assessment

A technique whereby peers or colleagues rate each others' performance. This is predicated on the belief that peers are in the best position to provide first-hand insights of someone's day-to-day behaviour.

Percentile Score

A score representing the percentage of scores in a sample that fall below it. For example, an applicant's score on a test at the 60th percentile indicates that 60 per cent of the scores of the other applicants are at this score or lower (e.g. if the 60th percentile represents a score of 25, then 60 per cent of applicants have scored 25 or less).

Personality Inventories	Measures designed to measure particular attributes of a person's disposition that are often used in selection procedures. Although many different theoretical approaches exist, most accept that the Big Five constructs – Extroversion, Introversion, Agreeableness, Conscientiousness, Openness to Experience – are the major structural components of personality.
Personnel Specification	A formal document derived from job analyses that states the skills and qualities required of successful applicants.
Polygraph	An instrument that measures physical symptoms of anxiety (e.g. increased perspiration, heart-rate, etc.). Commonly termed a 'lie detector'. In selection its intended purpose is to detect dishonest applicants. It is not very reliable, and its use for personnel selection is banned in the USA.
Positional Scoring System	Refers to the grading of an applicant in relation to others. Usually based on a Norm Table which shows how other people have previously scored on the same test or measure.
Predictive Validity (r)	A statistical coefficient reflecting the degree to which a selection test or method accurately predicts some specified aspect(s) of successful candidates' subsequent job performance (e.g. scores in a leaderless group discussion and the applicants' leadership behaviour in the job). Used in personnel selection utility analyses to calculate benefit/cost ratios.
Psychometrics	Measurement of psychological attributes. Includes mental testing in all its facets, such as intelligence, personality, aptitudes, abilities, etc.
Rating Scale	A scoring device used to assist in the rating of particular attributes.

Realistic Job Preview	Supplying an applicant with detailed realistic job information. Better informed candidates are less likely to leave when starting a job, and as such RJPs reduce the costs associated with turnover.
Reference	Information supplied by a 'third party'. Mostly used to verify accuracy of information supplied by applicant. Not very useful, unless focused on the characteristics of the job, highly structured and solicits facts rather than opinions.
Reliability	A generic term used to describe the dependability of a measurement device or test. In essence, the extent to which a selection method yields the same results when repeatedly used under similar conditions. The underlying principle is *consistency* of measurement. An important evaluative standard.
SD_y	The estimated cash value of one standard deviation of performance. Some research has indicated that SD_y approximates to 40 per cent of the wages paid for a particular job. Used in personnel selection utility analyses for calculating benefit/cost ratios.
Selection Method	A measurement device used to assess and guide the choice of candidates. The choice of appropriate selection methods should be derived from the important features of a job, identified from job analyses. Selection methods with good criterion-related validity include Assessment Centres, Structured Interviews, Work-Sample tests and Psychometric testing. Selection methods with relatively poor levels of criterion-related validity include Unstructured Interviews, References, Educational Qualifications, Graphology and Astrology.

Selection Procedure	Any selection method, combination of methods, or procedure used as a basis for an employment decision.
Selection Ratio	The ratio of jobs to applicants (e.g. four applicants for every job would provide a selection ratio of 0.25). Used to derive a standard performance score (Z_x) for use in personnel selection utility analyses, to calculate benefit/cost ratios.
Self-assessment	Direct estimates made by applicants about their own abilities or competencies. Usually judgements are based on comparisons with others.
Self-efficacy	Refers to judgements about 'how well one can execute courses of action required to deal with prospective situations'. Self-efficacy has been correlated with a wide range of work-related behaviour.
Situational Interview	A type of structured interview where the questions focus on applicants' future intentions. Based on goal-setting theory.
Standard Deviation (SD)	The square root of the mean square (variance) in a set of scores. In other words an indicator of the amount of spread in a set of scores from the mean.
Standard Score	A score that indicates where an applicant's scores lie in relation to the mean score of all the applicants on a particular test.
Stanine Score	A transformed standard score, with a mean of 5, a standard deviation of 2, with a range from 1 to 9.
Sten Score	A transformed standard score, with a mean of 5.5, and a standard deviation of 2, with a range of 1 to 10.

Supervisory Rating	An evaluation of some aspect(s) of a person's job performance conducted by his or her supervisor/manager.
T Score	A transformed standard score, with a mean of 50, and a standard deviation of 10, with a range of 20 to 80.
Tenure (t_r)	The average length of stay in any given job for existing job holders. Used in personnel selection utility analyses for calculating benefit/cost ratios.
Test–Retest Reliability	The correlation between the scores on the same test that is administered twice to the same people. It gives an indication of the test's stability over a period of time.
Trainability Test	A form of work-sample test involving structured and controlled learning periods. Mostly used to assess inexperienced applicants' potential for training.
Utility Analyses	A generic method for describing, predicting and explaining the usefulness or desirability of decision options, and analysing how that information can be used in decision-making. In personnel selection, used to calculate the benefit/cost ratio associated with a course of action, usually expressed as Quantity × Quality − Cost (i.e. $SD_y \times Z_x \times r \times t_r \times V_n - C$).
Work-sample Tests	Job-specific, simulated task-based selection methods, developed by incorporating samples of job behaviour into a practical selection test. Includes assessment-centre exercises (e.g. in-tray exercises, leaderless group discussions, etc.), typing tests, etc.
Z Score	A standard score with a mean of zero, and a standard deviation of one, with a range between plus and minus 3. Often used as basis for transformation to stanines, stens and T

scores (e.g. multiply Z by 10 and add 50 for a T score).

$\bar{Z}_x$ Standardized *performance* score, expressed in standard deviation units, derived from dividing the ordinate by the selection ratio. Used in utility analyses to calculate benefit/cost ratios.

References

Anderson, N. and Shackleton, V. (1990) 'Decision making in the graduate selection interview: A field study'. *Journal of Occupational Psychology*, **63**, 63–76.

Argote, L. and McGrath, J. E. (1993) 'Group processes in organization: Continuity and change'. In: C. L. Cooper and I. T. Robertson (eds) *International Review of Industrial and Organizational Psychology*, Vol. 8. Chichester: John Wiley.

Arvey, R. D. and Campion, J. E. (1982) 'The employment interview: A summary and review of recent literature'. *Personnel Psychology*, **35**, 281–322.

Asher, J. J. and Sciarrino, J. A. (1974) 'Realistic work-sample tests: A review' *Personnel Psychology*, **27**, 519–533.

Bandura, A. (1977) *Social Learning Theory*. Englewood Cliffs, NJ: Prentice-Hall.

Bandura, A. (1986) *Social Foundations of Thought and Action*. Englewood Cliffs, N.J.: Prentice-Hall.

Banks, M. H., Jackson, P. R., Stafford, E. M. and Warr, P. B. (1983) 'The job components inventory and the analysis of jobs requiring limited skill'. *Personnel Psychology*, **36**, 57–66.

Barrick, M. R and Mount, M. K. (1991) 'The Big Five personality dimensions and job performance: A meta-analysis'. *Personnel Psychology*, **44**, 1–26.

Bartram, D. A. (1994) 'Computer-based assessment'. In: C. L. Cooper and I. T. Robertson (eds) *International Review of Industrial and Organizational Psychology*, Vol. 9. Chichester: John Wiley.

Bartram, D. A. (ed.) (1995) *The Review of Personality Assessment Instruments (Level B) for Use in Occupational Testing*. Leicester: BPS Books.

Bartram, D. and Lindley, P. A. (1994) *Psychological Testing: The BPS 'Level A' Open Learning Programme*. Leicester: BPS Books.

Bartram, D., Lindley, P. A., Foster, J. and Marshall, L. (1990) *Review of Psychometric Tests for Assessment in Vocational Training*. Leicester: BPS Books.

Baxter, J. C., Brock, B., Hill, P. C. and Rozelle, R. M. (1981) 'Letters of recommendation: A question of value'. *Journal of Applied Psychology*, **66**, 296–301.

Bedford, T. (1988) 'Justifying the costs of assessment centres'. *Guidance and Assessment Review*, **4**, 1–3.

Belbin, R. M. (1981) *Management Teams: Why they Succeed or Fail*. London: Heinemann.

Ben-Shakhar, G. (1989) 'Non-conventional methods in personnel selection'. In: P. Herriot (ed.), *Assessment and Selection in Organizations*. Chichester: John Wiley.

Ben-Shakhar, G., Bar-Hillel, M., Bille, Y., Ben-Abba, E. and Flug, A. (1986) 'Can graphology predict occupational success? Two empirical studies and some methodological ruminations'. *Journal of Applied Psychology*, **71**, 645–653.

Bentler, P. M. (1989) *EQS Structural Equations Program Manual*. Los Angeles: BMDP Statistical Software.

Bethell-Fox, C. E. (1989) 'Psychological testing'. In: P. Herriot (ed.), *Assessment and Selection in Organizations: Methods and Practice for Recruitment and Appraisal*. Chichester: John Wiley, pp. 307–330.

Blum, M. L. and Naylor, J. C. (1968) *Industrial Psychology: Its Theoretical and Social Foundation*. New York: Harper and Row.

Boam, R. and Sparrow, P. (1992) *Designing and Achieving Competency*. London: McGraw-Hill.

Boudreau, J. W. (1989) 'Selection Utility Analysis: A review and agenda for future research'. In: J. M. Smith and I. T. Robertson (eds), *Advances in Selection and Assessment*. Chichester: John Wiley, pp. 227–257.

Boyatzis, R. E. (1982) *The Competent Manager: A Model for Effective Performance*. New York: John Wiley.

Brannick, M. T., Michaels, C. E. and Baker, D. P. (1989) 'Construct validity of in-basket scores'. *Journal of Applied Psychology*, **74**, 957–963.

Brinkman, J. A. (1983) 'Een klassifikatiesystem voor arbeidsanalyse-methoden'. (A classification system for job analyses methods). Technische Hogeschool, Eindhoven, Holland. Vakgroep Organisatie psychologie (Organizational Psychology Workgroup).

British Psychological Society (1993) *Graphology in Personnel Assessment*. Leicester: BPS.

British Psychological Society (1994) *Level B Standards in Occupational Testing*. Steering Committee on Test Standards. Information Pack. Leicester: BPS.

Brodt, S. E. (1990) 'Cognitive illusions and personnel management decisions'. In: C. L. Cooper and I. T. Robertson (eds), *International Review of Industrial and Organizational Psychology*, Vol. 5. Chichester: John Wiley.

Burt, C. (1940) *The Factors of Mind*. London: University of London Press.

Campion, J. E. (1972) 'Work sampling for personnel selection'. *Journal of Applied Psychology*, **56**, 40–44.

Campion, M. A., Pursell, E. D. and Brown, B. K. (1988) 'Structured interviewing: Raising the psychometric properties of the employment interview'. *Personnel Psychology*, **41**, 25–42.

Cascio, W. F. and Phillips, N. F. (1979) 'Performance testing: A rose among thorns?'. *Personnel Psychology*, **322**, 751–66.

Civil Service Commission (1987) *Review of Executive Officer Recruitment.* London: HMSO.

Cleary, T. A. (1968) 'Test bias: Prediction of grades of negro and white students in integrated colleges'. *Journal of Educational Measurement*, **5**, 115–124.

Conoley, J. C. and Kramer, J. J. (eds) (1989) *The Tenth Mental Measurements Yearbook.* Lincoln, Nebr.: Buros Institute of Mental Measurements.

Costa, P. T. and McCrae, R. R. (1985) *Manual for the NEO Personality Inventory.* Odessa, Fla.: Psychological Assessment Resources Inc.

Cronbach, L. J. (1951) 'Coefficient alpha and the internal structure of tests'. *Psychometrika*, **16**, 297–334.

Cronbach, L. J. and Glesser, G. C. (1965) *Psychological Tests and Personnel Decisions.* Urbana: University of Illinois Press.

Cronbach, L. J. and Meehl, P. E. (1955) 'Construct validity in psychological tests'. *Psychological Bulletin*, **52**(4), 281–302.

Cureton, E. E. (1971) 'The stability coefficient'. *Educational and Psychological Measurement*, **31**, 45–55.

Development Dimensions (1975) *Catalogue of Assessment and Development Exercises.* Pittsburgh: Development Dimension.

Dobson, P. (1989) 'Reference reports'. In: P. Herriot (ed.), *Assessment and Selection in Organizations.* Chichester: John Wiley.

Downs, S. (1968) 'Selecting the older trainee: A pilot study of trainability tests'. *National Institute of Industrial Psychology Bulletin*, 19–26.

Downs, S. (1985) *Testing Trainability.* NFER-Nelson Personnel Library, Windsor.

Drakeley, R. J. (1989) 'Biographical Data'. In: P. Herriot (ed.), *Assessment and Selection in Organizations: Methods and Practice for Recruitment and Appraisal.* Chichester: John Wiley, pp. 439–454.

Drakeley, R., Herriot, P. and Jones, A. (1988) 'Biographical data, training success and turnover'. *Journal of Occupational Psychology*, **61**, 145–152.

Drucker, P. (1986) *The Frontiers of Management.* New York: Dutton.

Dulewicz, V. (1989) 'Assessment centres as the route to competence'. *Personnel Management*, November, 56–59.

Edwards, A. G. and Armitage, P. (1992) 'An experiment to test the discriminating ability of graphologists'. *Personality and Individual Differences*, **13**, 69–74.

Eysenck, H. J. and Nias, D. K. B. (1982) *Astrology: Science or Superstition?* London: Temple Smith.

Fay, C. H. and Latham, G. P. (1982) 'Effects of training and rating scales on rating errors'. *Personnel Psychology*, **35**, 105–16.

Feltham, R. (1989) *Assessment centres.* In: P. Herriot (ed.) *Assessment and Selection in Organizations: Methods and Practice for Recruitment and Appraisal.* Chichester: John Wiley, pp. 439–454.

Ferguson, E. and Cox, T. (1993) 'Exploratory factor analysis: A user's guide'. *International Journal of Selection and Assessment*, 1, 84–94.

Fine, S. A. and Wiley, W. W. (1977) *An Introduction to Job Analysis*. Kalamazoo, Mich.: Upjohn Institute for Employment Research.

Flanagan, J. C. (1954) 'The critical incident technique'. *Psychological Bulletin*, 52, 327–358.

Fletcher, C. (1991) 'Candidates' reactions to assessment centres and their outcomes: A longitudinal study'. *Journal of Occupational Psychology*, 64, 117–127.

Furnham, A., Steele, H. and Pendleton, D. (1993) 'A psychometric assessment of the Belbin Team-Role Self-Perception Inventory'. *Journal of Occupational and Organizational Psychology*, 66, 259–260.

Gaugler, B. and Thornton, G. C. (1989) 'Number of assessment center dimensions as a determinant of assessor accuracy'. *Journal of Applied Psychology*, 74, 611–618.

Gaugler, B., Rosenthal, D. B., Thornton, G. C. and Bentson, C. (1987) 'Meta-analysis of assessment center validity'. *Journal of Applied Psychology*, 72, 493–511.

Gauquelin, M. (1978) *Cosmic Influences on Human Behavior*, 2nd edn. New York: AST.

Gauquelin, M. (1980) *Spheres of Destiny*. London: Dent.

Gauquelin, M., Gauquelin, F. and Eysenck, S. B. G. (1979) 'Personality and position of the planets at birth: An empirical study'. *British Journal of Social and Clinical Psychology*, 18, 71–5.

Gough, H. G. (1984) 'A managerial potential scale for the California Psychological Inventory'. *Journal of Applied Psychology*, 69, 233–240.

Guerrier, Y. and Riley, M. (1992) 'Management assessment centres as a focus for change'. *Personnel Review*, 21, 24–31.

Guilford, J. P. and Fruchter, B. (1978) *Fundamental Statistics in Psychology and Education*. New York: McGraw-Hill.

Harris, M. M. and Schaubroeck, J. (1988) 'A meta-analysis of self–supervisor, self–peer, and peer–supervisor ratings', *Personnel Psychology*, 41, 43–62.

Heneman, R. L., Wexley, K. N. and Moore, M. L. (1987) 'Performance-rating accuracy: A critical review'. *Journal of Business Review*, 15, 431–448.

Herriot, P. (1981) 'Towards an attributional theory of the selection interview', *Journal of Occupational Psychology*, 54, 165–73.

Herriot, P. (1989) *Recruitment in the Nineties*. London: IPM.

Herriot, P. and Rothwell, C. (1981) 'Organizational choice and decision theory. Effects of employers' literature and selection interview'. *Journal of Occupational Psychology*, 54, 17–31.

Hesketh, B. and Robertson, I. T. (1993) 'Validating personnel selection: A process model for research and practice'. *International Journal of Selection and Assessment*, 1, 3–17.

Hill, S. (1991) 'How do you manage a flexible firm? The total quality model'. *Work, Employment and Society*, 5, 397–415.

Hogan, J. and Quigley, A. M. (1986) 'Physical standards for employment and the courts'. *American Psychologist*, **41**, 1193–1217.

Hogan, J., Hogan, R. and Busch, C. M. (1984) 'How to measure service orientation'. *Journal of Applied Psychology*, **69**, 167–173.

Horn, R. (1991) 'MAILBOX: a computerized in-basket task for use in personnel selection'. *European Review of Applied Psychology*, **41**, 325–328.

Hough, L. M., Eaton, N. K., Dunnette, M. D., Kamp, J. D. and McCloy, R. A. (1990) 'Criterion-related validities of personality constructs and the effects of response distortion on those validities'. *Journal of Applied Psychology*, **75**, 581–595.

Howard, G. S. and Dailey, P. R. (1979) 'Response-shift bias: A source of contamination of self report measures'. *Journal of Applied Psychology*, **62**, 144–50.

Hunter, J. E. and Hirsh, H. R. (1987) 'Applications of meta-analysis'. In: C. L. Cooper and I. T. Robertson (eds), *International Review of Industrial and Organizational Psychology*, Vol. 2. Chichester: John Wiley.

Hunter, J. E. and Hunter, R. F. (1984) 'Validity and utility of alternative predictors of job performance'. *Psychological Bulletin*, **96**, 72–98.

Hunter, J. E. and Schmidt, F. L. (1982) 'Fitting people to jobs: The impact of personnel selection on national productivity'. In: M. D. Dunnette and E. A. Fleishman (eds), *Human Performance and Productivity*, Vol. 1. Hillsdale, N.J:. Earlbaum.

Hunter, J. E. and Schmidt, F. L. (1990) *Methods of Meta-Analyses: Correcting Error and Bias in Research Findings*. Beverly Hills, Calif.: Sage.

Iles, P. A. and Robertson, I. T. (1995) 'The impact of personnel selection and assessment procedures on candidates'. In: P. Herriot and N. Anderson (eds), *Assessment and Selection in Organizations*. Chichester: John Wiley.

Institute of Personnel Management (1994) *Graphology Information Note.* London: IPM.

Janz, T. (1989a) 'The patterned behaviour description interview: The best prophet of the future is the past'. In: R. W. Eder and G. R. Ferris (eds), *The Employment Interview: Theory, Research and Practice*, Beverly Hills, Calif.: Sage, pp. 158–168.

Janz, T. (1989b) 'Case study on Utility: Utility to the rescue, a case of staffing program decision support'. In: J. M. Smith, and I. T. Robertson (eds), *Advances in Selection and Assessment*. Chichester: John Wiley, pp. 269–272.

Jenkins, R. (1986) *Racism and Recruitment: Managers, Organizations and Equal Opportunity in the Labour Market*. Cambridge: Cambridge University Press.

Jeswald, T. A. (1977) 'Issues in establishing an assessment center'. In: J. L. Moses and W. C. Byham (eds), *Applying the Assessment Center Method*. New York: Pergamon.

Jones, A. (1988) 'A case study in utility analysis'. *Guidance and Assessment Review*, **4**, 3–6.

Jones, A. and Harrison, E. (1982) 'Prediction of performance in initial officer training using reference reports'. *Journal of Occupational Psychology*, **55**, 35–42.

Joreskog, K. G. and Sorbom, D. (1988) *LISREL 7, A Guide to the Program and Application*. Chicago: SPSS.

Kandola, R. S. (1989) 'Using job analysis as a basis for selection'. In: J. M. Smith and I. T. Robertson (eds). Chichester: John Wiley. *Advances in Selection and Assessment*. pp. 43–45.

Kellet, D., Fletcher, S., Callen, A. and Geary, B. (1994) 'Fair testing: The case of British Rail'. *The Psychologist: The Bulletin of the British Psychological Society*, Jan., pp. 26–29.

Kelley, H. H. and Michela, J. L. (1980) 'Attribution theory and research'. *Annual Review of Psychology*, **31**, 457–501.

Klimoski, R. J. and Rafaeli, A. (1983) 'Inferring personal qualities through handwriting analysis'. *Journal of Occupational Psychology*, **56**, 191–202.

Kohn, M. L. and Schooler, C. (1982) 'Job conditions and personality: A longitudinal assessment of their reciprocal effects'. *American Journal of Sociology*, **87**, 1257–1286.

Kuder, G. F. and Richardson, M. W. (1937) 'The theory of estimation of test reliability'. *Psychometrika*, **2**, 151–160.

Latham, G. P. (1989) 'The reliability, validity and practicality of the situational interview'. In: R. W. Eder and G. R. Ferris. *The Employment Interview: Theory, Research and Practice*. Newbury Park, Calif.: Sage.

Latham, G. P. and Saari, L. M. (1984) 'Do people do what they say? Further studies on the situational interview'. *Journal of Applied Psychology*, **69**, 569–573.

Latham, G. P. and Wexley, K. N. (1977) 'Behavioural observation scales for performance appraisal purposes'. *Personnel Psychology*, **30**, 255–268.

Latham, G. P. and Wexley, K. N. (1981) *Increasing Productivity through Performance Appraisal*. Reading, Mass.: Addison-Wesley.

Levine, E. L. (1983) *Everything you Wanted to Know about Job Analysis*. Tampa, Fla.: Mariner Publishing.

Lewis, C. (1985) *Employee Selection*. London: Hutchinson.

Locke, E. A. and Latham, G. P. (1990) *A Theory of Goal-setting and Task Performance*. London: Prentice-Hall.

London, M. and Hakel, M. (1974) 'Effects of applicant stereotype, order and information on interview impressions'. *Journal of Applied Psychology*, **59**, 157–162.

Love, K. G. (1981) 'Comparison of peer assessment methods: Reliability, validity, friendship, and user reaction'. *Journal of Applied Psychology*, **66**, 451–457.

McCormick, E. J. (1976) 'Job and task analysis'. In: M. D. Dunnette (ed.), *Handbook of Industrial and Organizational Psychology*. Chicago: Rand-McNally.

McCormick, E. J., Jeaneret, P. R. and Mecham, R. C. (1972) 'A study of job characteristics and job dimensions based on the Position Analysis Questionnaire (PAQ)'. *Journal of Applied Psychology*, **36**, 347–368.

McDaniel, M. A., Whetzel, D. L., Schmidt, F. L. and Maurer, S. D. (1994)

'The validity of employment interviews: A comprehensive review and meta-analysis'. *Journal of Applied Psychology*, **79**, 599–616.

McLeod, D. (1994) cited in 'Graphology in business'. *Management Today*, Oct.: pp. 17.

McNeil, B. J., Pauker, S. G., Sox, H. C. Jr. and Tversky, A. (1988) 'On the elicitation of preferences for alternative therapies'. In: H. R. Arkes and K. R. Hammond (eds), *Judgement and Decision Making: An Interdisciplinary Reader*. New York: Cambridge University Press.

Management Charter Initiative (1990) *Summary Report on Personal Competence Project*. London: MCI.

Mayo, J., White, O. and Eyesnck, H. J. (1977) 'An empirical study of the relation between astrological factors and personality'. *Journal of Social Psychology*, 105, 229–36.

Merrit-Haston, R. and Wexley, K. N. (1983) 'Educational requirements: Legality and validity'. *Personnel Psychology*, **36**, 743–753.

Miller, S. (1984) *Experimental Design and Statistics*, (2nd edn), New Essential Psychology Series. London: Methuen.

Moe, K. O. and Zeiss, A. M. (1982) 'Measuring self-efficacy expectations for social skills: A methodological enquiry'. *Cognitive Therapy and Research*, **6**, 191–205.

Moorman, R. H. and Podsakoff, P. M. (1992) 'A meta-analytic review and empirical test of the potential confounding effects of social desirability response sets in organizational behaviour research'. *Journal of Organizational and Occupational Psychology*, **65**, 131–149.

Mosel, J. N. and Goheen, H. W. (1982) 'Agreement among replies to an employment recommendation questionnaire'. *American Psychologist*, **7**, 365–366.

Mosier, C. I. (1947) 'A critical examination of the concepts of face validity'. *Educational and Psychological Measurement*, **7**, 191–205.

Muchinsky, P. M. (1979) 'The use of reference reports in personnel selection: A review and evaluation', *Journal of Occupational Psychology*, **52**, 287–297.

Mumford, M. D., Stokes, G. S., Owens, W. A. and Sparks, C. P. (1991) 'Development determinants of individual action: Theory and practice in the application of background data measures'. In: M. D. Dunnette (ed.), *Handbook of Industrial and Organizational Psychology*, (2nd edn). Orlando, Fla.: Consulting Psychologist Press.

Murphy, K. R. (1988) 'Psychological measurement: Abilities and skills'. In C.L. Cooper and I.T. Robertson (eds), *International Review of Industrial and Organizational Psychology*, vol 3. Chichester: John Wiley.

Neiner, A. G. and Owens, W. A. (1982) 'Relationships between two sets of biodata with 7 years separation'. *Journal of Applied Psychology*, **67**, 146–50.

Nisbett, R. E. and Ross, L. (1980) *Human Inference: Strategies and Shortcomings of Social Judgment*. Englewood Cliffs, NJ.: Prentice-Hall.

North, D. (1994) 'Using educational qualifications to discriminate between people: Is it safe?'. Paper presented at the Annual British Psychological

Society, Occupational Psychology Conference, Birmingham, Jan. 3–5.

Ones, D. S., Viswesvaran, C. and Schmidt, F. L. (1993) 'Comprehensive meta-analysis of integrity test validities: Findings and implications for personnel selection and theories of job performance'. *Journal of Applied Psychology*, **78**, 679–703.

Paulhaus, D. L. (1989) 'Socially desirable responding: Some new solutions to old problems'. In: D. M. Buss and N. Cantor (eds), *Personality Psychology: Recent Trends and Emerging Directions*. New York: Springer.

Payne, T., Anderson, N. and Smith, T. (1992) 'Assessment centres, selection systems and cost-effectiveness: An evaluative case study'. *Personnel Review*, **21**, 48–56.

Penney, G. and Lazzarini, A. J. (1979) *Data-Processing Staff Selection – A Validation Study*. Manchester: NCC.

Pursell, E. D., Dossett, D. L. and Latham, G. P. (1980) 'Obtaining valid predictors by minimizing rating errors'. *Personnel Psychology*, **33**, 91–96.

Reilly, R. R. and Chao, G. T. (1982) 'Validity and fairness of some alternative employee selection procedures'. *Personnel Psychology*, **35**, 1–62.

Robertson, I. T. (1993) 'Personality assessment and personnel selection'. *European Review of Applied Psychology*, **43**, 187–194.

Robertson, I. T. (1994) 'Personality and personnel selection'. In: C. L. Cooper and D. M. Rousseau (eds), *Trends in Organizational Behaviour*. Chichester: John Wiley.

Robertson, I. T. and Downs, S. (1989) 'Work sample tests of trainability: A meta-analysis'. *Journal of Applied Psychology*, **74**, 402–410.

Robertson, I. T. and Kandola, R. S. (1982) 'Work sample tests: Validity, adverse impact and applicant reaction' *Journal of Occupational Psychology*, **55**, 171–83.

Robertson, I. T. and Kinder, A. (1993) 'Personality and job competencies: The criterion-related validity of some personality variables'. *Journal of Occupational and Organizational Psychology*, **66**, 225–244.

Robertson, I. T. and Makin, P. J. (1986) 'Management selection in Britain: A survey and critique'. *Journal of Occupational Psychology*, **59**, 49–57.

Robertson, I. T. and Sadri, G. (1993) 'Managerial self-efficacy and managerial performance'. *British Journal of Management*, **4**, 37–45.

Robertson, I. T., Gratton, L. and Sharpley, D. (1987) 'The psychometric properties and design of assessment centres: Dimensions into exercises won't go'. *Journal of Occupational Psychology*, **60**, 187–195.

Robertson, I. T., Gratton, L. and Rout, U. (1990) The validity of situational interviews for administrative jobs'. *Journal of Organizational Behaviour*, **11**, 69–76.

Robertson, I. T., Iles, P. A., Gratton, L. and Sharpley, D. (1991) 'The impact of personnel selection and assessment methods on candidates'. *Human Relations*, **44**, 963–982.

Roe, R. A. (1984) 'Advances in performance modelling: The case of validity generalisation'. Paper presented at the symposium 'Advances in

Testing'. Acapulco, Mexico, Sept. 6.
Roe, R. A. (1989) 'Designing selection procedures'. In: P. Herriot (ed.), *Assessment and Selection in Organizations: Methods and Practice for Recruitment and Appraisal*. Chichester: John Wiley, pp. 127–142.
Roe, R. A. and Grueter, M. J. M. (1989) 'Developments in personnel selection methodology'. In: R. K. Hambleton and J. Zaal (eds), *Advances in Testing*. Deventer: Kluwer.
Ross, L. and Anderson, C. (1982) 'Shortcomings in the attribution process: On the origins and maintenance of erroneous social assessments'. In: D. Kahneman, P. Slovic and A. Tversky (eds), *Judgment under Uncertainty: Heuristics and Biases*. New York: Cambridge University Press.
Sackett, P. R. and Dreher, F. F. (1982) 'Constructs and assessment centre dimensions: Some troubling empirical findings'. *Journal of Applied Psychology*, **67**, 401–410.
Sadri, G. and Robertson, I. T. (1993) 'Self-efficacy and work-related behaviour: A review and meta-analysis'. *Applied Psychology: An International Review*, **42**, 139–152.
Saville and Holdsworth Ltd (1985) *Occupational Personality Questionnaire Manual* (updated in 1990). Esher, Surrey: Saville and Holdsworth.
Saville and Holdsworth Ltd (1988) *WPS Manual* (updated 1995). Esher, Surrey: Saville and Holdsworth.
Schmitt, N. and Coyle, B. W. (1976) 'Applicant decisions in the employment interview'. *Journal of Applied Psychology*, **61**, 184–192.
Schmitt, N. and Noe, R. A. (1986) 'Personnel selection and equal employment opportunity. In: C. L. Cooper and I. T. Robertson (eds), *International Review of Industrial and Organizational Psychology 1986*. Chichester: John Wiley.
Schmitt, N. and Ostroff, C. (1986) 'Operationalizing the "behavioral consistency" approach: Selection test development based on a content-oriented strategy'. *Personnel Psychology*, **39**, 91–108.
Schmitt, N., Gooding, R. Z., Noe, R. A. and Kirsch, M. (1984) 'Meta-analyses of validity studies published between 1964 and 1982 and the investigation of study characteristics'. *Personnel Psychology*, **37**, 407–22.
Schuler, H. and Funke, U. (1989) 'The interview as a multimodal procedure'. In: R. W. Eder and G. R. Ferris (eds), *The Employment Interview: Theory, Research and Practice*. Newbury Park, Calif.: Sage, pp. 183–192.
Schuler, H. and Moser, K. (1995) 'The validity of the multimodal interview'. *German Journal of Work and Organizational Psychology*, **39**, 2–12. (In German).
Schuler, H., Funke, U., Moser, K. and Donat, M. (In press) *Personnel Selection in R & D: Aptitudes and Performance of Scientists and Engineers*. Göttingen: Hogrefe. (In German).
Schwab, D., Heneman, H. G. and DeCottis, T. A. (1975) 'Behaviorally anchored rating scales: A review of the literature'. *Personnel Psychology*, **28**, 549–62.
Scribner, S. (1986) 'Thinking in action: Some characteristics of practical

thought'. In: R. J. Sternberg and R. K. Wagner, *Practical Intelligence.* Cambridge: Cambridge University Press.

Shackleton, V. J. and Newell, S. (1991) 'A comparative survey of methods used in top British and French companies'. *Journal of Occupational Psychology.* **64**, 23–36.

Smith, J. M. and Abrahamsen, M. (1992) 'Patterns of selection in six countries'. *The Psychologist: Bulletin of the British Psychological Society,* **5**, 205–207.

Smith, J. M. and Robertson, I. T. (1993) *The Theory and Practice of Systematic Personnel Selection,* (2nd edn). Basingstoke: Macmillan.

Smith, P. L. and Kendall, L. M. (1963) 'Retranslation of expectations: An approach to the construction of unambiguous anchors for rating scales'. *Journal of Applied Psychology,* **47**, 149–155.

Spearman, C. (1927) *The Abilities of Man.* London: Macmillan.

Spector, P. E., Brannick, M. T. and Coovert, M. D. (1989) 'Job analysis'. In: C. L. Cooper and I. T. Robertson (eds), *International Review of Industrial and Organizational Psychology,* **4**. Chichester: John Wiley.

Squires, P., Torkel, S. J., Smither, J. W. and Ingate, M. R. (1991) 'Validity and generalizability of a role-play test to select telemarketing representatives'. *Journal of Occupational Psychology,* **64**, 37–47.

Stahl, M. J. (1983) 'Achievement, power and managerial motivation: Selecting managerial talent with the job choice exercise'. *Personnel Psychology,* **36**, 775–789.

Sternberg, R. J. and Wagner, R. K. (1986) *Practical Intelligence.* Cambridge: Cambridge University Press.

Stewart, R. (1967) *Managers and their Jobs.* London: Macmillan.

Stokes, G. S. and Reddy, S. (1992) 'The use of background data in organizational decisions'. In: C. L. Cooper and I. T. Robertson (eds), *International Review of Industrial and Organizational Psychology,* Vol. 7. London: John Wiley, pp. 285–322.

Stokes, G. S., Hogan, J. B. and Snell, A. F. (1993) 'Comparability of incumbent and applicant samples for the development of biodata keys: The influence of social desirability'. *Personnel Psychology,* **46**, 739–762.

Tett, R. P., Jackson, D. N. and Rothstein, M. (1991) 'Personality measures as predictors of job performance: A meta-analytic review'. *Personnel Psychology,* **44**, 703–742.

Thornton, G. C. and Byham, W. C. (1982) *Assessment Centers and Managerial Performance.* New York: Academic Press.

Tversky, A. and Kahneman, D. (1988) 'Rational choice and the framing of decisions'. In: D. Bell, H. Raiffa and A. Tversky (eds), *Decision Making: Descriptive, Normative and Prescriptive Interactions.* New York: Cambridge University Press.

Vernon, P. E. (1961) *The Structure of Human Abilities,* 2nd edn. London: Methuen.

Wall, T. D. and Martin, R. (1987) 'Job and work design'. In: C. L. Cooper and I. T. Robertson (eds), *International Review of Industrial and Organizational Psychology,* Vol. 2. Chichester: John Wiley.

Williams, A. P. O. and Dobson, P. M. (1987) *The Validation of the Regular Commission Board*. Army Personnel Research Establishment, Jan.

Woodruffe, C. (1990) *Assessment Centres*. London: IPM.

Woolley, R. M. and Hakstian, A. R. (1992) 'An examination of the construct validity of personality-based and overt measures of integrity'. *Educational and Psychological Measurement*, **52**, 475–489.

Zdep, S. M. and Weaver, H. B. (1967) 'The graphoanalytic approach to selecting life insurance salesmen'. *Journal of Applied Psychology*, **51**, 295–299.

—— *Index*